SAILING THROUGH GOOD TIMES AND BAD

ROY SAMUELS

2010

SAILING THROUGH GOOD TIMES AND BAD
BY ROY SAMUELS

ISBN 978-1-4467-9840-9

CONTENTS

ACKNOWLEDGEMENTS

When my Grandson Tony telephoned me just over two years ago and said; 'The English teacher (at King David School Manchester) has asked me to produce an essay on my Grandparents early life and times I little realised where the call would lead me.

Having furnished him with a page or two of historical details I got to think about my own Grandparents and realised how little I knew of their early lives, coming from diverse traditions and backgrounds. When I asked several friends what they knew of their grandparents and family roots most had little or no knowledge. So, there and then, I decided to put on record for whoever might wish to learn what life was like in Dublin and Liverpool before, during and after World War II: a period of 20 years for my Family and me. This of course was the subjective view of a child growing into maturity. You, dear reader will appreciate that all biographies are personal accounts with inevitable shades of bias and therefore, if over three books certain of my recalled memories and opinions clash with yours, I am sorry.

Following immediately with a second book "Sailing through the Jungle" again covering two decades 1953 - 1973 and containing stories of my work experiences in the world of fashion I was greatly assisted by my Sons :Colin, who has by now along with this publication spent many hours editing all three books. Without his patient input I could not have managed to complete the trilogy in a relatively short space of time; and to Ian, yet another word of gratitude for running a sharp eye over the initial proofs.

Once more I wish to thank my Wife Anita and Sons Colin, Peter, Ian, Neal, for their encouragement during the writing of this book with loving, helpful and moral support: the same support that also lifted my spirits when I was diagnosed with leukaemia in 2002. Over recent years I am also indebted to those wonderful medical people who helped me cope with the illness so well that between treatment days I have managed to live an almost normal life assisting my Sons in business, painting, and of course, writing.

To Professor John L. Yin, Doctors David Osbourne and Peter Holman (San Diego), Martin Rowlands, along with the kind helpful nurses at the North Manchester Hospital, the Royal Manchester Infirmary and Alexandra Hospital, a special word of thanks.

More recently, I am grateful for additional advice and treatment from Doctors Ellen Gockle and John Kok Shun.

Each of my three biographical books have been titled with the leading word "SAILING". The reason is simply this, I have looked upon life as a journey, similar in a way to a sea adventure. As such my years and experiences have seen me encounter all sorts of weather fair and foul, sunshine and rain.

Along the way I have been most fortunate to start out with the affectionate guidance of two great parents and dear Melvyn the best Brother a guy could have. Through childhood and school days I had a good teacher in Joseph Barron and gained three of the best pals Abe Baker, Willy Malkinson and Dave Solomons. We all joined scouts where Scout-leaders Leslie Silverstone, Ralph Morris, Joe Jay Levey and Maurice Gordon introduced and inspired us for many years in a fabulous youth movement.

Later, on life's voyage, I learned at work the disciplines and benefits to be gained by reaching the highest standards of skills required for whatever the job entailed. In this area I was indebted to factory manager Alf Solomons and business director Sam Scheps.

When I entered the uncharted waters of running my own business, I was lucky to have two of the best assistants an employer could wish for Anna (Nance) Butcher and Linda (Moore) Collie. I am happy to say even now, many years on, both remain excellent friends: two caring and reliable people.

As one can see from the above lines, in casting my mind back over the years I am constantly reminded of how much I owe to every Family member, relative and friend, those who stood by my side through life's calm seas and turbulent storms, men and women, near or afar, chums who can on any point of contact reconnect our warm close ties, hence the title of this book

"Sailing Through Good Times and Bad"

Front cover:
Liner - Queen Elizabeth 2
Oil painting Roy Samuels, 2009

INTRODUCTION

1973

A time before we all had Lap-Top Computers, Mobile Telephones, to spend hours - Texting, Twittering, Googling, Facebooking, Skype-ing ...

It was a year of shocks. The kind of year when the media have a ball, running with one gloom and doom story after another. That is not to say it's the carrier of bad news who is entirely to blame for what we're fed in word and print. The public have an insatiable appetite for reports of disasters, killings, scandal, or any other form of sad and bad happenings. So, the media feed the masses with what they crave.

In the U.S.A. two newspaper reporters working for the Washington Post uncovered what became known as the Watergate affair and of President Richard Nixon's 'Whitewash' attempt. Nixon denied any mis-handling of facts but as the story ran and ran, it became clear he was implicated in a massive cover-up. Tagged with the nick-name - 'Tricky Dickie,' he was impeached the following Summer and forced into retirement ... succeeded by Gerald Ford who became the 38th President of the U.S.A.

The political scene in Ireland saw big changes. Erskine Childers replaced Eamonn DeValera as President and Liam Cosgrave's party Fine Gael, ousted the Fianna Fail party and formed a coalition government with the smaller Labour party. The Irish economy was in poor shape and many college graduates took their diplomas and made for foreign shores. It was said back then ... before the term Celtic Tiger was born, that the country's biggest export was young promising talent.

Early in the year, the U.K. was shaken by an IRA bombing campaign that began in London, spreading later to nearby military sites. After 4 years of killings and destruction in Northern Ireland, the IRA adopted new tactics, bringing terror to mainland Britain. This, despite a Northern Ireland referendum of the time which showed 591,820 citizens in favour of retaining links with Britain and only 6,468 for links with the the Republic.

On the high seas the country drifted into another war ... with Iceland! It began when the Icelandic government unilaterally increased its territorial waters from 12 to 50 miles, thereby depriving British trawlers from fishing in rich Cod fields. This storm in a fish bowl was titled The Cod War. For once Britain failed to rule the waves. With far greater naval resources, the Royal Navy could have destroyed the Icelandic gun boats in a day, but in the eyes of the world such an action would have damaged the country's reputation.

With other major counties around the globe handling upheavals of one sort or another, all were about to face the greatest economic damage since World War Two.

It began in October, when Egypt and Syria attacked Israel on the holiest day in the Jewish calender ... Yom Kippur. Within minutes of the first sirens howling across the nation, soldiers, sailors, airmen and all auxiliary service personnel rushed to their reporting stations where they were ordered to join their regular units in strategic places, to repel the advancing invaders.

Within three days of heavy combat the Israeli forces not only stopped the advance but began to overpower huge numbers of well equipped forces ... armed with the Soviet Union's latest and most sophisticated weaponry.

A week after the invasion Israel's forces were poised to cross the Suez Canal and head towards Cairo. At this stage the Russians, not wanting to see their customers annihilated put pressure on America, threatening to become engaged in the war unless they persuaded Israel to stop fighting. Bluff or not the Americans thought it best to avoid a more major conflict and did as they were asked.

It was now ... after the hostilities ceased that the Arab oil producers rose up with sanctions against Western countries. Because the U.S.A. was friendly towards Israel any country friendly with the Americans was deemed to be aligned with Israel. Not exactly true in all cases but that's how the Arab nations saw things. Overnight, Iran doubled the price of oil, followed immediately by Saudi Arabia and other Middle-Eastern producers. On top of this oil production was greatly reduced bringing many economies to a point of collapse. In Britain and Ireland massive motor service station queues formed with long lines of 50 cars a common sight. In Britain, ration books for petrol were issued and a ban imposed on cars travelling over 50 miles per hour.

Electrical power supplies were cut, forcing the majority of businesses to operate a three day working week. To aggravate the grim situation the British miners, in pursuit of a wage increase, refused to work overtime. This led to a confrontation with Ted Heath's Tory led government. It was a battle the Prime Minister lost.

Adding to the above misery interest rates rose to over 11% and unlike 2008 and 2009 when some governments threw money at the crisis of the time in order to 'stimulate' their economies the 1970's depression was allowed to fester and limp along. If a lucky few of my contemporaries have forgotten that cold bleak period then I reckon they were well cushioned in ways beyond most citizens.

In 2008 the collapse of confidence in many banks due to over-trading practices and failure to operate in a responsible manner may be unique to that period's economic downturn, but in general many more people were badly affected by the economic crisis that ran through the early/mid seventies. Then, unemployment rose sharply in Britain from 1,000,000 to over 3,000,000 in 1977. By comparison in 2008 the total number of people out of work reached 2,600,000. This figure was expected to stretch towards 3.2 million in 2009. Instead, by the end of 2009 the total began to decrease. I realise that this is no comfort to anyone who was made redundant in recent times but with all the media hype I want to get some figures in perspective.

The above picture was the background setting as I sailed out to embark upon a new business venture. Not the best of timing. Similarly in 2008, when my cousins Jackie and Maurice also took a major business change of direction Maurice wryly said -
"We're expanding into a recession!"

Like 2008/9 the overall scene for 1973 could best be summed up by Captain Boyle one of the characters in Sean O'Casey's play Juno and the Paycock when he said -

"The whole World's in a state of Chassis"

That, dear reader, is probably as reasonable an introduction to 1973 as you're ever likely to get.

CHAPTER 1

TOYS WHOLESALE

The Introduction to this, my third book, coincidentally places me in a time of World economic slowdown, similar to the events described in the opening chapters of book 1 (1933-1953) and book 2 (1953-1973).

In 1933 it was my newly wed Parents who faced the rigours of coping in hard times and in 1953 just as I sailed along without a care I too found myself facing a series of tough problems. I've often described these unexpected setbacks as akin to walking into an unseen plate-glass door. The metaphorical door lies in one's path, but pre-occupied, the walker crashes into it with a clanging sound - BEDANG! So it is with life. We gaily go about our day to day chores and leisure periods not spotting the doors until we hit them full tilt.

One important event did not come upon us unexpectedly. It was Colin's Barmitzvah. During the preceding 12 months Anita and I prepared for the occasion. At one stage Colin was attending a privately run Hebrew class under the supervision of Miss Rebecca Gavron, the same person who taught me 28 years earlier. Sadly within weeks it became obvious the teacher, now well on in years, was struggling to cope.

To ensure Colin was well prepared to recite a portion of the Torah (Sacred Scroll) we approached another Hebrew teacher Cyril Rifkin to take Colin under his wing for private lessons. I knew Cyril well. As youngsters we lived two doors apart and I spent many hours playing in his home with younger brother Philip.

The weekend programme for the celebration was after the Sabbath service during which Colin would take his place at the centre of the congregation and chant a portion of the scriptures. There was to be a reception at the Adelaide Road Synagogue hall for all present. This followed by a luncheon for 90 family members, friends and children. For the evening we planned a catered reception at home inviting just over 40 adults, again mostly family and close friends.

All the catering was ably handled by Annie Danker, a hard working wonderful lady. Annie was a communal institution. For decades this much respected woman, a pint-sized bundle of energy, with a loyal team of cooks, kitchen helpers and waitresses, organised Weddings, special celebratory functions, Barmitzvahs and private parties at prices that could not have provided her with much profit. Many people of my generation still remember her walking around cleared dining tables and with a smile asking was everything alright?"

To our relief, all our hopes and plans were fully realised. Colin, now at the age of 13 was in the eyes of the Jewish religion accepted as a man, responsible for his own actions. On Barmitzvah day he performed his role and duty to perfection, a big credit to him and Cyril Rifkin. Now, after all the excitement, we had a breather of about 12 months before planning for Peter's big day!

After 20 years in the ladies fashion wear business, described in book 2, I decided on a complete change of scene. The idea for a new venture came to me in bed one night shortly after my head hit the pillow. Having seen how well my Parents were doing in their retail toy shop, it struck me that there must be a reasonably good living to be made with a wholesale toy supply company. Even with tight household budgets most parents and adult relations will see children get the best and latest toys and games.

The planning and preparation for the new toy firm took far less time than the previous fashion business. The set-up costs were also minimal by comparison. One of my first decisions was to give the company a name. Nothing fancy, just an easy title to remember, not to be confused with a competitor. With that in mind I brought up the subject at the weekend when visiting my Parents. With their knowledge of who's who in the toy trade it seemed a logical step. In addition, my Mother had an excellent knowledge of English and a way of finding the right sounding word for any occasion or item. Some of her selected names came in a roundabout fashion, such as that chosen for their retail toy shop. When thinking of a title my Mother Ellen, sometimes called Nel, read a report in the Daily Express about a woman living in Camberely, Surrey who caused a commotion every morning in the town centre when serenely walking a rather large pack of dogs along the busy pavements. Dog leads became entangled with shoppers feet and the air filled with angry shouts and yelps. Shopkeepers and townspeople tried to have CAMBERLEY NEL as she became known banned from taking her morning 'doggie' stroll. The story amused my Mother and she quickly decided upon calling the toy shop Camberlys As you may notice, she dropped the second letter E for the business.

Faced with my request for a suggested name for the wholesale company, she came up with a shortened version of Camberly 'Cambie'. I tried the name out on several people and it seemed to go down well.

My Father offered to exchange cars with me on work days, his estate for my saloon. This was to enable me to ferry goods in and out. All I required now were goods to sell. Well, it wasn't just as simple as that. Clearly I first identified the type of retail customer to approach and at what price level. To help the cash flow and build up a quick and varied stock I decided on offering very keen prices for payments on delivery. To enable me do this and retain a decent profit between purchase and sale I had to buy at the lowest price possible. So, armed with only a modest sized roll of bank notes I headed for a reputable toy importer on the North side of Dublin. The firm exclusively sold to the wholesale trade and it took me some time to convince them that I was a new bona fide wholesale trader. Once my account details were accepted and ability to pay cash up front noted we got down to discussing cost prices. As soon as I discovered they had different prices for different sized orders my years of buying in the clothing business came in to play. Having established a list of prices for my selection I then did as one of our American customers had done, asking for lower prices based on larger purchase amounts. Haggling over and assisted by a warehouse worker I happily filled the estate with my first purchased cartons of inexpensive toys.

That same evening Da gave me the benefit of his judgement on values. For example, instead of thinking how much should I charge the retailer he worked the following formula: Reckoning on the perceived RETAIL value for each item he set down the shop's recommended selling price. Then working back from that figure and after calculating the retailer's mark-up margin he arrived at a suitable price for me to charge. The recipe could hardly fail. Once we were confident a toy was good value at a certain price and were able to assure the retailer of a good profit success was on the cards.

Next morning, I drove the toy laden estate to the North side of Dublin, around the bay area and later to the satellite towns of Santry, Swords and Sutton. At each stop I made an on-the-spot cash sale, returning in the evening with an almost empty car. Twenty-four hours later, I'd collected another estate load of toys and headed South, this time along the coast, stopping at every suitable shop until once more the stock sold out. With just Miss Butcher keeping track of the paperwork back in the office the weeks went by with me acting as buyer, delivery man and salesman. By now I was venturing further afield and trying at the same time to service the earlier buyers with repeat orders. It was exhausting, exhilarating heady stuff and I enjoyed every minute.

By the end of 1974 some daily selling trips were stretching to 120 miles. Not a huge distance, but, when taking the stop and selling times into account the day lengthened considerably. The majority of shop owners did the buying and on the whole I found them more grounded than those in the fashion world and easier to get on with.

People being people I did come across the odd-bod, mostly in circumstances I found funny. On the last leg of a long trip I stopped at Newbridge, a town about 25 miles south of Dublin. The shop owner was an elderly woman of erratic behaviour. On this call her daughter, a very pleasant 25 year old, dealt with me. After making her selection from my box of samples, she said; “By the time you bring in the stock, I may be gone, if so, my mother will pay you”.

The estate was parked close to the shop and as I walked to the tailgate there was a loud clap of thunder and the heavens opened with a deluge of rain. Caught without a jacket, my shirt and trousers were drenched in seconds. The freak burst of rain, like a dam burst, passed quickly but I was thoroughly soaked. Returning to the shop under a heavy carton, I elbowed my way past the entrance door and was met with a loud shout - “You're drenching the shop!”

It came from the shop owner. A smallish wispy woman of about 65 years stood behind the main counter pointing to a trail of floor puddles. She had the face of someone who scowled a lot, tight lips drawn down at the edges and a glare that made one wonder if she ever smiled. Placing the large box on a back counter I turned to apologise. With hair plastered to my head and a skin clinging soaked shirt, I said -
“I'm sorry, but it's been raining hard out there.”

She glanced out of the window and snorted - “No it's not ... That's sunshine out there, so it is”. I wasn't going to argue. “Like I said Mam ... I'm sorry”
“What are ye doin' here and what's in the box”?
“Toys I answered quietly.”
She went to the carton but it was too tall for her to peer into. Still annoyed, she said in a crabby high pitched voice,“I didn't order toys”.

“These were ordered by your daughter” I replied, handing her the bill. She snatched my handwritten invoice and with money from a tin box below the counter, flung the cash towards me. Some notes slid across the glass top and landed by my feet. I bent down to recover the money, then said “Thank you. You know lady, I work hard for a living, you shouldn't throw money at me or anyone else for that matter.”

“I did not throw the money and let me tell you somethin', you're the cheekiest van driver I've ever come across”!
When I got behind the wheel of the car I burst out laughing. Me! another job description title to my growing list. From the age of 14 I had progressed from a messenger boy who began his apprenticeship sweeping floors in a furriers to a top fur-cutter, fashion trade manager, business consultant, toy wholesaler, all the way down in seconds, to - 'cheeky van driver'! The brief encounter was like a scene from Alice's Adventures in Wonderland.

On other trips I had to find time to chat with the shop owner and in some cases, a wife or husband or even a retired father. Having completed my business I could never show I was in a hurry to move on to the next call. “So ... what route did you take today”? I might get asked. In response to my reply the owner's father would 'tut-tut' giving me the benefit of his county knowledge with an alternative set of directions.

“The next time you come by ... take the xxxx road or the yyyy or zzzz by-pass”. With the women ... it was a case of me enquiring after members of the family. “How did Mike or Sean or Marie fare with their exam results”?

My calls were almost like social visits. News of other tradespeople were swapped, road and weather conditions compared, trivia to some or as I liked to think, bonding ties between salesperson and buyer.

The Western economies sank further into chaos during 1974 and '75. The Arab oil states reduction of oil output resulted in higher prices and this of course damaged many industries. In Britain and Ireland we had crippling strikes coming on top of the energy shortages. Ireland's national bus company went on what the public called 'the annual bus strike' and British miners sank Ted Heath's Tory led government with a total walk out. Inflation ran into double figures, hitting 25% by 1975. The word 'crisis' was frequently overused by the newspaper banner writers as week after week more grim news came to light. With unemployment rising the British Labour party, under the leadership of Harold Wilson, came into power. One of his first actions was to seek a loan from the IMF who first insisted the government cut back severely on public spending. Both Britain and Ireland were forced into major cutbacks, the British slashing health service and education costs. Left-wingers in the Labour party were infuriated but, saddled with heavy debts, the government had no alternative.

With severe Winter power-cuts 'Which?' magazine offered some light-hearted advice, telling its readers: “The simplest answer may be to use a torch to light your way to bed and stay there until it blows over”.

So dreadful were the energy cuts, more cynical views suggested it was the prevailing conditions that caused the infamous Lord Lucan to disappear! To digress ... For those who may have forgotten the 'Lord Lucan affair', or are too young to know the story here is a brief on the disappearance of Lord Lucan:

In November of 1974, Countess Lucan staggered into a pub in London's Belgravia seeking refuge, saying she had been attacked by her husband who had murdered the children's nanny. The battered body of Sandra Rivett was found shortly after by the police in the Lucan's home basement. Of Lord Lucan there was no sign. The Lucans had separated after a bitter marriage and with mounting debts due to heavy gambling it was generally believed that in a fit of temper he went to kill his wife but in the dark killed the nanny by mistake. A coroner's court found Lucan guilty of murder but no trial could take place without the accused, who was never found. Over the years there were reports of the Earl being seen in Australia and South Africa but like the missing racehorse Shergar, Lord Lucan's disappearance remains a mystery.

Through the year we still went to the 'flics'. Back then there were eight or so cinemas in the city centre. The big crowd-pullers were The Sting with Paul Newman, Robert Redford and Robert Shaw, The Godfather starring Marlon Brando, Robert DeNero, Robert Duvall and Diane Keaton, Day of the Jackal with Edward Fox and Cyril Cusack. All brilliant movies. In each film there was a good plot with superb actors, films that still entertain audiences 40-50 years on. Only a week ago Anita and I watched 'The Godfather' again after a period of many years and were held with interest right the way through. Brando's performance was tremendous. The film, though long, moved at a spanking pace, capturing well the mood of the Mafia scene as it probably was in the mid nineteen hundreds.

CHAPTER 2

BE PREPARED

I joined the Scout movement at the age of 11 in 1944 and thanks to the excellent leaders of the day was fired with enthusiasm. The 16th Dublin (Jewish) Troop was one of the country's most active units and part of the 16th Group. A group that included a Wolf Cub Pack and for older Scouts the Rover Crew. In total there were about 100 members. The Group leader was Maurice (Morrie) Gordon. In charge of the Scout Troop were Scoutmaster Leslie Silverstone and Assistant Ralph Morris. Leslie, an excellent motivator in my life, was a man I admired greatly. The Rover Crew was led by another wonderful individual, a charismatic Scot named Joe J. Levey. All these that I've named inspired many young people and I hope there are leaders like them in the scouting movement today.

Not only did these four men play a large part in my early life and development but also became good friends. Sadly, of the times I write, the mid 70's, Joe J. Levey had passed away and as some say in scouting 'gone to join the Great Scoutmaster of all Scouts'. His vivacious daughter Vivienne who was in the Girl Guide movement with Anita now lives in California and keeps in touch with us with regular calls and emails.

In my days within the 16th troop as a scout I reached the highest position, that of Senior Patrol Leader. Encouraged by Morrie Gordon, my friends Abe Baker, Willy Malkinson and Davy Solomons, all fellow patrol leaders decided to move with me from the troop to the Rover Crew. Under the wings of Joe J. Levey and Senior Rover mates Monty Ross and Mendel Stein I stayed involved with the 16th for many years. In fact from then on I never broke my association with the Group. This leads me to now explain why I've hearkened back to earlier scouting days.

A day in November 1974, the telephone rang. The slight American accent at the other end of the line instantly told me it was Mister Gordon. Even as adults none of my generation ever addressed him other than Mister G. or Mister Gordon.

"Roy, in November 1975 the 16th Scout Group will be 50 years old. I'm calling on Leslie (Silverstone), Ralph (Morris), Monty (Ross), Richard (Stein) and you to form a 'Friends of Scouting Jubilee Committee'. Three of the ex-Cub lady leaders have agreed to help; Naomi Taylor, Barbara Feldman and Joy Gafson. What I have in mind for discussion is a Grand Celebration, an impressive dinner at the Shelbourne Hotel (Dublin's oldest premier hotel) inviting the Chief Scout and other special guests with speeches and a Scout show to follow. Morrie was a great sales person but he didn't have to work hard on any of us. For anything to do with the 16th we were ready and willing to help, just as we had always done, with present day leaders on Scout Gang Shows and other events. At the first 'Jubilee' meeting a group of very enthusiastic 'oldies' assembled and soon rolled back the years remembering and recounting events until Mister G. brought us to order.

On our first of many meetings it was agreed that Leslie and I assisted by Naomi and Leslie's wife Sybil, would be responsible for putting together a commemorative magazine. This to include a history of the 16th along with various tales of yore, letters from overseas ex-members and a host of photographs. With advertisements and sponsors it would also raise a lot of cash. Here is a brief extract from a 'Letter from the Magazine Editors', in which I described our quest as - "not the beginning of a task, but a journey."

The journey took our small team around the world and spanned fifty years, seeking names, compiling facts, sifting stories and discovering old photographs. We walked, sat, wrote, talked and laughed our way through hills of information and make no mistake, we indulged ourselves to the hilt. The ready response to our feelers was overwhelming and material for our magazine poured in. The information gleaned owed much to the memories of some of our 'old boys' and if any details do not quite match the memory of others we apologise in advance.

At one of our sub-committee meetings, Leslie suggested we offer a few sample news clips on how the world looked from Dublin in 1925. So, off I went to the Central Library in Kildare Street and searched through back copies of the Irish Times and Dublin Evening Mail. There were few world shattering reports to be found but here is a cross selection of the items we ran in the magazine.

“Modern ballroom dancing is frivolous, graceless and inartistic, and the music is awful”, said Madame Pavlola who is touring Ireland at present.

22 LEFT OUT OF 500
TRAGEDY OF A ZIONIST
PILGRIMAGE.
Jerusalem (by mail)

News has been received here by the Palestine Zionist Executive of the arrival of a small party of Zionist pilgrims, the remnants of some 500 who started from Kiev for Palestine. The greater part of the journey was made on foot, many of the pilgrims were arrested by the Soviet authorities and some were exiled to Siberia. A large number were imprisoned at Baku and a not inconsiderable number must have fallen by the wayside. The Zionist authorities are seeking the secure recognition of these pilgrims as political refugees while the consul is demanding their extradition to Russia.

CIVIL AVIATION IN IRELAND
POSSIBILITIES OF THE NEAR FUTURE

Two Bristol Fighter Aeroplanes, the first contingent of a flight of six similar machines arrived at Baldonnell aerodrome on Saturday last. The machines fitted with a 275 H.P. Rolls Royce engine have a cruising speed of 100 miles an hour and are capable of a maximum speed of 120 miles an hour.

The population in the Irish Free State was estimated in June of this year to be 3,163,000. (About 4,500,000 in 2009).

A FAST FORD

Alleged to have driven a motor car at thirty-four miles an hour, John McCarthy, Gratton Hotel, Dublin, who appeared at Dundrum District Court yesterday, said that the summons came to him as - a bolt out of the blue. He did think that he could go at such a speed.
District Justice Reddon - "What kind of car"?
McCarthy - "Eh an old Ford".
The Justice - "Eh well, you never know what they can do (laughter) fined 15 shillings (75p)".

Among some of the newspaper advertisements I came across the following offers:

```
Gilbeys Scotch 70l bottles  s12/6   (60p)
Gilbeys Gin ..............  s13/-   (65p)
White Lily cigarettes 10 pk, 6d     (2.5p)
Ford Coupe                 £195
Chrysler Four              £335
Donnybrook, 8 roomed house £950
US Dollar $4.845 to £1.00
```

1925 Scout census details -

Scout Officers	36
Cub Officers	33
Rovers	119
Scouts	514
Cubs	307

Lady Baden Powell (Chief Guide) paid a first official visit to Dublin and attended a great rally at the Mansion House inspecting the companies numbering about 1,000.

Two of the big films showing in Dublin back in 1925 were:
Metropole Cinema: 'Little Annie Rooney' starring Mary Pickford.
Stella Cinema: 'The Thief of Baghdad' with Douglas Fairbanks.

The first Cub Scout to enrol in the 16th Dublin was Ralph Morris who at this time of writing in 2009 celebrated his 83rd birthday a few months ago. To my knowledge, Ralph is the last surviving member of those who joined in 1925. From abroad we had a huge number of letters enquiring about the 50th celebrations.

They came from all over Britain, with many from the U.S.A. Australia, Canada and Israel. There were quite a few from South Africa and even some from Switzerland, Jamaica and The Bahamas. All the messages expressed fond thoughts of their days in the 16th with wonderful recounted tales of scouting memories.

My meetings with Leslie were great fun. Being older, he could delve back further than I, for personal reminiscences and with a terrific sense of humour highlight those incidents that most 'old boys' want to hear of again. Along with several others we also interviewed Jackie Bloom, an ex-scout who was the first member of the 16th to be awarded the 'King Scout' badge. By 1938 there were six King Scouts in the troop. Apart from working with Jack when he was employed in his father's fur business, I well remember him as a Rover Scout. One weekend, while camping on the Rover site in Powerscourt I watched him use a felling axe, splitting logs with graceful sweeps. I thought at the time; when I grow to his height I'd like to be as expert an axeman as Jack.

When we called on him he was more than pleased to relate a few scouting stories. That was after he first showed us some of his oil paintings. Knowing of my interest in that field we took up half the evening swapping notes. His work, strong bright colours, was in the style of the Irish painter Jack Butler Yeats.

In a matter of weeks Leslie and I felt we'd been around the world; one-to-one interviews, telephone calls, letters, and best of all discovering where some of the ex-Pats had got to. For me especially, working on the project was a great relief from business. Another distraction was when Monty Ross reminded us that in line with the 50th Anniversary Morrie Gordon would have served 40 years scouting with the Group and suggested the committee prepare a presentation to mark that achievement.

After a few floated ideas for a suitable surprise gift Monty came up with the solution: “Roy will paint an appropriate scene to mark Morrie's service”.

Flattered though I was, I tried to think of something else but in seconds everyone else had moved on to discuss another topic. In a Dublin idiom, Monty was saying “Roy ... ye're elected”!

CHAPTER 3

REGULAR TOYS

What do I mean by - 'Regular Toys'?
Well, back in the 1970s and beyond most toys ... and I mean most toys, were not 'character linked'. There were a few Micky Mouse figures and wind-ups, Pinocchio string puppets, James Bond, Batman, Thunderbirds die-cast model cars and rocket type vehicles but not until 1975 did character merchandising really take off. It was the film Star Wars in 1975 that launched toys into a new era. Shortly before the film was released in Dublin my Father showed me an invitation both he and Ma received from a major toy distributor. It was to a private reception and showing of the film for toy retailers. The presentation was a precursor to a product launch. He had not heard of the film and asked if I thought he should go. Having read some American reviews I had a reasonable grasp of the film's storyline and thought it would indeed promote 'Star Wars' toy sales.

It was a mid-day reception at the Adelphi cinema, one of Dublin's finest, now sadly gone. I covered in the shop during my folks absence. I can still see my Father's expression on their return. "Nice reception with plenty of sales ballyhoo but don't ask me what the film was about."

Da seldom went to the cinema so I wasn't really surprised to hear he found the plot 'convoluted'. However, it did not prevent him ordering the toy replicas. Nonetheless, it was a cautious opening order and at the end of a long sales campaign by the makers he proved right. The film itself was a huge box office success but despite what many people believe toy sales failed to hit the expected targets.

An amusing by-line to the above film; Sir Alec Guinness, who played the part of Ben Kenobi was offered initially a sum of money for his work. Knowing there was a tight budget for the film he graciously opted instead to accept a small percentage of any profit that might be made. His kind offer was welcomed. To his and everyones' amazement Star Wars proved to be one of the greatest money spinners ever! His earnings on that film alone ran into millions, far more than most actors earn in a lifetime.

In the wholesale toy trade I was now well established in most towns and resorts within a 70 mile radius of Dublin. The bulk of my selection were Hong Kong toys, at the low priced end of the market. I needed to expand into better quality and higher priced products. With that in mind I visited the Harrogate Toy Fair, the biggest of its kind in the U.K. Inside two days I placed orders with five well established manufacturers. This was for Nurse, Cowboy and Indian playsuits die-cast Trucks, Board games, Plush teddy-bears and a big range of guns. The interesting thing about the guns was we stocked seven replica models, selling thousands in a year. Later, in years to come at the height of the violence in Northern Ireland I decided we should drop these items from our sales list. Two guns in particular the Colt 45 and Luger were very real looking. We were the first company to take this step.

With the additional lines the orders were growing and although Da was helping me with deliveries I was falling behind on calls. The higher priced merchandise boosted profits but were bulkier, taking up more space in the estate car. The vehicle having served me well was now far too small for the business. Something bigger was required and a full-time driver. My Father, who was 68 and tormented at times with varicose veins had done trojan work. By a stroke of good fortune I discovered my Father's butchering assistant Tommy Connelly was out of work. Tommy, same age as myself, was the first messenger boy hired by Da. When I approached and offered him a job as van driver he was delighted. So, with a new Toyota Hi-Ace van and driver, we were able to increase sales substantially. Tommy was the most loyal and hard working person an employer could wish for. Both he and Miss Butcher were dependable and never baulked at busy times when extra time and effort was required. As soon as I could afford to I took steps to organise a private pension for both. The benefits of which came into effect on their 65th birthdays.

Right through 1975 Britain and Ireland suffered one economic crisis after another. Unemployment was still rising and in the U.K. The Chancellor imposed strict wage control, freezing all incomes of £8,500 and over. Similar wage caps were applied in Ireland. Still, my Parents, Brother Melvyn and wife Avril, along with Cambie, all managed to make money. Talking with Melvyn one day, he said "Always important to remember; in every boom there are firms that go bust and in every downturn there are businesses that forge ahead."

On a similar theme there is the story of a reporter's interview with the racing car champion Jackie Stewart. He was asked; what was his immediate on-track reaction to a car crash, where the race was allowed to continue.
"I press harder on the accelerator", he replied to the surprised man.
"But, are you not tempted to slow because of the incident, worried about what other dangers might lie ahead"?
"No, other drivers may slow and that's when I'll take the opportunity to speed by".

November came and with it the long planned for Golden Jubilee dinner marking the occasion of the 16th Dublin Scout Troop's 50th anniversary. The gala evening was held at the Shelbourne Hotel where Group leader Maurice (Morrie) Gordon with wife Ray, along with section leaders, welcomed the guests at a cocktail reception.

Among the invited visitors were Chief Scout, Commander T. McKenna, Scout Commissioner Dick Tennant, Chief Rabbi Dr. Cohen, Rabbi Aloney and founder Scoutmaster of the 16th George Morris.

It proved to be a huge success with many overseas past members joining in the celebrations. Old and not so old faces exchanged old and not so true reminiscences. As the wine and words flowed, behind the scenes a well drilled team of organisers moved events smoothly along. Seniors Ralph Morris and Gerry Alexander had practised and drilled for weeks with their 'walkie talkies' in order to co-ordinate their actions. I witnessed a marvellous moment when Ralph tried to communicate urgently with Gerry.

On the balcony, overlooking the ballroom, Ralph knelt on one knee peering through a rail and crouched like a wartime soldier or reporter under fire called up his team mate for immediate assistance:
"Hello Gerry ... This is Ralph calling ... over!"
There was no response, so again and again he tried, just as a valiant operator would do in a tight situation or aboard a stricken vessel.
"Come in Gerry ... Ralph needing you urgently ... over."
"Gerry ... please answer ... urgent ... over."
"Gerry ... CAN YOU HEAR ME? ... OVER"
Suddenly there came a loud reply:
"Yes Ralph ... now I can hear you ... loud and clearly."
"Thank goodness Gerry ... you're sounding so near too. Where are you ...over ?"
"Standing with Roy ... right behind you"!

Following the dinner, toasts and speeches, there was a loud fanfare as a massive brilliantly lit decorated cake was wheeled in. The inscription read -
50 YEARS - 16th DUBLIN TROOP.

The Chief Scout's wife Mrs McKenna and Morrie Gordon had the joint honour of blowing out the candles. This was a signal for our floor manager Jackie Bloom and Ralph Morris to commence the stage show with Scouts and Cubs performing. A few brief acts were then followed by a campfire with Jack leading the audience into all the familiar songs. Finally 'TAPS'.

To also mark the 50th a tree was planted on the Group Scout site at Powerscourt Enniskerry, County Wicklow, by Irish President O'Dalaigh.

Ten years later Morrie Gordon would once again call upon his loyal team of 'old boys' this time to help organise a celebratory 60th Anniversary bash!

Scout Reunion Committee

Ralph Morris, Richard Gordon, Barbara (Berber) Feldman, Roy Samuels, Leslie Silverstone
Morrie Gordon, Naomi Taylor, Richard Stein, Joy Gafson, Benny Marks

Throughout my reminiscences I've touched on extreme periods of weather, long before we had experts warning us of impending doom: the Summer of 1939 and in complete contrast the Winter 0f 1946-47, one of the coldest, most prolonged in living memory. In late January the temperature dropped to 20°F, even the River Thames froze. The 'Big Freeze' lasted to the end of March and ran the coal mines down to zero stocks. Thousands of farm animals perished in the unrelenting cold conditions. In Ireland many lakes and canals froze over for the first time in living memory. A few wealthy people used to holidaying in Winter resorts, delighted with the conditions, went ice skating.

It was natural for people to speculate on the prospects of a coming ice age. I cannot remember what timing the forecasters put on this impending period. In 1952 flash floods during the middle of August devastated the town of Lynmouth killing 34 people. A worse disaster occurred in December when London ground to a standstill with 'Smog' a mix of chimney smoke and fog. The noxious cloud hung over the capital city for nearly a week killing 4,000-5,000 people. Returning to the 1970s, the Summer of 1976 scuttled most estimates for the coming of another ice-age. About the middle of June the temperature began to steadily rise. It reached 32°C and remained around that level for weeks. With no rain farmland dried out and many reservoirs emptied. Hose pipe bans were strictly imposed and in Britain a minister was appointed to co-ordinate supplies and rationing. In parts of South-West England, Wales and as far North as Yorkshire people queued in the streets for water. There was an old joke many years ago about a young student from India studying at Eton. In a letter home, he wrote of a strange and impressive English custom which he had just witnessed. “Men dressed all in white come on to a field and after placing some sticks in the ground one man throws a red ball at another man who tries to hit it with a flat club. Immediately the heavens open and great rains fall”. And that is what happened in August when the first Test match at Lord's cricket ground began. The crowd cheered louder than usual.

The ending of the severe water shortage was not the end of Britain's problems. About this time Britain's new Prime Minister James Callaghan, who had succeeded Labour leader Harold Wilson, faced a financial meltdown. I'm telling this story for one reason only. It is to compare Callaghan's view of handling a money crisis with that of Gordon Brown. As we know in 2009 Brown borrowed billions in order to deal with a recession but in 1976 Callaghan made a long speech to the Labour Party conference. Read how differently he viewed and handled things then:
"We used to think that you could spend your way out of a recession and increase employment by cutting taxes and boosting government spending. I tell you with candour, that option no longer exists".

In the run-up to Christmas my parents shop was getting busier and busier. With most of my seasonal orders fulfilled I was in a position to lend a hand serving customers. I never ceased to be amazed by the amount of money people spent on children. One of the 'hot' toys for boys that year was a remote controlled articulated truck. This vehicle was about 15 inches (35cm) in length. Large stores engaged demonstrators to display the toy, it's various manoeuvres; detaching the cab from the truck and so on. The de-luxe model sold for £85, an expensive toy then. On a busy Saturday two parents with a young boy of about seven approached me and asked quietly so the youngster shouldn't hear; "How much is the artic. truck in the shop window". Pointing to a shelf, I replied out of the child's earshot; "Eighty-five pounds".

They looked at each other and I knew the price was higher than they expected. Dressed poorly, I guessed they might welcome a more keenly priced item. Quickly I drew their attention to another section with similar trucks, slightly smaller.

“These perform the same moves and cost £65, that's £20 less.”

Again, the couple exchanged glances. This time, the mother walked back to the larger model and bent over the child, pointing. “That's what you want Santa to bring son, isn't it”? The boy nodded and whispered, “Yes”.

With that, the father winked and said, “Right, if that's what he wants then that's what Santa will bring him”.

As the mother drew her son away the father made the purchase and arranged to pick up the toy at a later date. It was all to do with peer pressure. Come Christmas the boy would not feel overshadowed by his friends' new possessions from Santa.

From the month of June onwards the toy shop ran a 'Christmas Club' whereby customers could put aside items and pay over time whatever amounts they wished, whenever it suited them and at no extra cost. This facility also allowed buyers to add newer toys, as seen on television, to their selection. Many customers ran bills close to a thousand pounds and the storage room bulged with hundreds of parcels. To give some idea of numbers sold in a particular item Camberlys outsold every other shop and store in toy Forts. Between Desert Forts and Medieval Castles they sold well over a thousand models. Not only that but their selection of soldiers ran into tens of thousands. It wasn't only soldiers either. The list of play figures was huge. British infantry, British 8th Army, American infantry, German infantry, German Africa Korps, Japanese infantry, British Household Guards, Mounted Life Guards, Mounted Royal Guards, Battle of Waterloo British and French mounted and foot soldiers. English Crusaders, on foot and mounted, French Legionnaires, Arab and Turkish fighters, Cowboys and Indians both on foot and mounted, U.S. Cavalry and Confederates. All these figures came posed in different positions. Along with tents, wigwams, teepees, log cabins, tanks, field guns, army ambulances, motor bike riders, there was a big selection of other small accessories.

When my Father had time he spent ages with some customers showing them how to create a total scene, setting out the figures, helping them make a selection that made sense. For example some people, without guidance, picked a number of cowboys mixed with Arabs or Turks! One such customer came to me one day, not sure which figures should be matched with others. This well dressed woman in her late-fifties volunteered in the course of making a selection that the purchase was for a grandson.

Then, when we had almost agreed a total number, she hesitated and said "You know, this seems such a shame, when I have three boxes of perfect soldiers at home. I bought them for my son when he was a child but he showed no interest whatsoever and they've remained in the original boxes."
"When did you buy them"? I asked.
"Well, he's thirty seven now, so it must be over thirty years ago".
"Are they in good condition"? I asked again.
"Untouched. They are still fixed in their boxes. Red coats, you know, guardsmen, some playing instruments.
In reply to a third question she gave me a rough guess as to how many toy soldiers were involved. At this, I said "It's not because I want to complete this sale but take my advice, don't give those boxed sets to your grandson. Are you planning a trip to London in the near future"?
She smiled nodding "Yes, as it happens I'm going there next week".
"Then do yourself a favour, take the boxes and have Sothebys or Christies value them.
The woman laughed. "Are you joking"?
"No I'm serious. Whatever the reason for your London trip, don't

miss a good opportunity for a valuation".
Highly amused the woman completed her purchase and within days I forgot about the episode. Weeks went by until one day a woman sought me out on the shop floor.

She gave me a friendly "Hello" in a somewhat familiar way that puzzled me. Then she said, "Don't you remember me? You suggested a while ago that I have Sothebys value boxed sets of toy soldiers". I immediately recalled the meeting.
"Well, I did as you said and guess what? They gave me a total valuation of almost two thousand pounds"!

Remember, this was 1977! Although I expected they were worthy of keeping and worth a goodly sum of money, I was pleasantly surprised and delighted for her. To show her appreciation she made a top-up selection adding to the grandson's collection. Perhaps the grandson, having missed out on playing with his father's soldiers, was later presented with or inherited the boxed sets!

In addition to detailing at length the wide variety of soldier type play figures I could equally fill a lot of space on other products that featured a wealth of accessories. Items such as Barbie Doll, Action Man, Model Trains and of course Lego. Every one a popular toy with most children. What surprises me here in 2009 is that many yesteryear toys are still played with, despite the big interest in hand-held electronic games. Even board games like Chess, Scrabble, Monopoly, Cluedo, still sell well. What has changed greatly is the number of toys and games children own today. Bedrooms and playrooms stacked with everything I've mentioned plus teddy bears, dolls, playhouses and the "must have" newest branded toy, usually based on the latest full length cartoon or computer generated film. Shrek and Wall E are just two examples. The Disney shops offer an amazing selection of cartoon branded goods, a parent's nightmare if accompanied by a child, or worse still, several children!

Among boys of all ages, a widely popular game was 'Subbuteo' a table-top football game. Enthusiasts bought not only their own favourite teams but popular continental and international squads. Leagues were formed in most towns and I remember seeing exhibition games on television. After many years of good sales Subbuteo sales shrank to a trickle. This may have been due to the massive rise in live football broadcasts on television. No indoor replicated version of football could compete with the real thing.

Television may have affected badly the sales of Subbuteo but it must have enhanced a growing interest in car racing. Created in the 1950s Scalextric became a big seller and in 2009 it still sells well. Now owned by the model train maker Hornby both products continue to capture the imagination of the young and old. Hornby after selling off Meccano to a French company then took over Airfix and is now a highly successful model supply firm.

Although I mentioned earlier people commenced ordering and storing toys early for Christmas, the Camberlys shop always experienced a massive late rush on Christmas Eve. In Britain retail sales tailed off shortly after lunch-time but in Dublin it was very different. Panic buying usually began around four o'clock and by six frustrated shoppers ended up grabbing whatever was left. Camberlys could not close the doors until seven at the earliest. The actual deadline was determined by what my Father called “The Silly Hour”. This was the moment when a tired individual rushed in and enquired ... “Do you sell oven trays”? or some other bizarre item never found in a toy store.
“It's time to close” Da would announce.
“Get the shutters down and the remaining customers served quickly”.

Shop closed, it became a tradition over the years for Family and Staff to head to a nearby restaurant for dinner where a pre-arranged booking had been made. It was a pleasant and relaxing way to unwind after the most hectic sales day in the calendar.

4

ANTIQUES AND A NEW DAWNING

In 1977 the BBC launched a new television series called 'The Antiques Roadshow'. The planners anticipated it would run for one season. Thirty-three years later it is still one of the most popular programmes, now shown all around the world. Anita and I are not avid TV watchers, have never watched Coronation Street, Holby City, Eastenders, Big Brother, Sex & the City or any other similar long running soap. For us as with a lot of our friends the 'Antique' show is a must watch programme.

At the beginning the main presenter was an affable roly-poly expert named Arthur Negus, In our minds he seemed to be involved over many years and it was a surprise to discover recently that he only participated in the show for six years. Soon after it began David Battie and Hilary Kay joined the team of experts and both are still giving their opinions and valuations. To anyone who has lived over 40-50 years it is fascinating to discover what values are placed on items that were discarded only decades ago. Very often, we hear someone say "Did you see on the 'Antiques Show' the valuation given on that old teddy bear, doll or 'Dinky' model car"? Everyone who watches that series has said at one time or another "I had one of those years ago, if only I held on to it"! Ah yes, we've all thrown out valuable items or did we?

Although certain old items have increased in value because of their beauty or scarcity other things have diminished. Whatever the reason it boils down to supply and demand. Just because something is old won't guarantee a huge price. A week ago two wealthy bidders at a London auction went hammer and tongs over a metal figure sculptured by 'Alberto Giacommetti'. The clinching bid was

£65,000,000! I watched two art experts discuss this event and when asked what their personal valuation was on the piece both were reluctant to say. As one ventured to suggest, any work of art coming up to auction will be affected by the strength or weakness of interest in those seeking to own the item. A puzzling fact that came to light during the above chat, was that at the time when Giacommetti cast the black sculpture he actually produced three (or it may have been a total of four) figures ... exactly the same! Asked why then one statue should reach such a massive figure he shrugged and said, "You are are talking about an auction in which two big billionaires with big egos went head to head, neither prepared to be beaten on the day"!

For anyone interested in making an offer on one of the other statues the experts said they were probably valued somewhere between 25-30 million pounds. A bargain!

Moving on into 1978, two new developments took place:

In July, the first ever 'Test Tube' baby was born in Manchester. Louise Brown weighed in at 5.12lbs (2.61kg) and with mother Lesley, were in excellent health after a caesarean section delivery. It was so big an event at the time one of the tabloid newspapers paid £300,000 for the mother's story. The research leading to this new way of helping women with blocked fallopian tubes took 12 years and was carried out by doctors Patrick Steptoe and Robert Edwards. Until his death 10 years later Steptoe kept a close observation on all similar procedures ensuring there were no post-birth problems.

Love them or, love them less the 'Cordless' telephone came into vogue, firstly in Japan followed swiftly by eager buyers in the United States. Men and women say of one another "Can't live with them... can't live without them".

The same might be said of the mobile 'phone. According to statistics in the Western World there are more of these instruments than there are people! The claim sounds a wee bit exaggerated, but then it might be that some people are beginning to maintain several telephone accounts as they do with credit cards!

A new way of assassination came to light in September. Early reports of a Bulgarian being stabbed by an umbrella in broad daylight on the streets of London sounded too far-fetched to believe. Over a period of days a tale of dark deeds equal to any novel thriller by Anthony Horowitz gradually built up into a full scale international dispute. The victim, Georgi Markov, was an employee of Radio Free Europe a station I'd never heard of. As such he used his position to attack the Bulgarian communist regime. Most East European communist countries of the time did not take kindly to any form of criticism and so poor Mr. Markov was murdered. Standing in a bus queue at a busy stop in Aldwych he felt a sharp pain in his thigh. On looking around he saw a man with an umbrella running away. The attacker, it was discovered later, was a known Bulgarian secret agent. Within hours the victim was admitted into hospital with a high fever. It was then the medics discovered a puncture mark on his thigh. Three days later Markov died. According to the coroner, a metal pellet had been stabbed (from an umbrella) at close range into the skin which inflicted a poison into the bloodstream. I told you this had all the ingredients of a thriller.

Soon after this happening another account came to light, of a Bulgarian exile living in Paris who suffered a similar attack upon leaving a Metro station. Fortunately this man survived.

Above, I mentioned the writer Anthony Horowitz. One could write a book about him. Born into a wealthy family in Stanmore near London, his early life was so unreal, even he looks back with regrets;

a mansion of a home surrounded with nannies, chauffeurs and servants. He was packed off to a boarding school at the age of eight. His millionaire father got into a financial mess and in order to avoid losing the greater part of his fortune transferred money to other accounts. In the midst of his hide-away transactions the man died and to this day no one has been able to trace where the bulk of his fortune went. If the father was something of an odd bod, well I believe it was nothing to compare with one of Anthony's grandmothers who gave him a torrid time. In his own words he came to hate her. When Horowitz reached his 14th birthday he became aware of a certain Bond, James Bond. From then on, with a fired imagination he began dreaming up his own adventure stories of Alex Rider and today many exploits of Alex Rider, British secret agent with M16, may be found on most booksellers shelves. Among Horowitz's best sellers are titles like Stormbreaker, Point Blank, Eagle Strike and coming out shortly Snakehead.

Apart from his excellent books, Horowitz is one of Britain's busiest writers and has written television episodes of Poirot, Midsomer Murders, Murder most Horrid and Foyle's War'.

Anita and I have probably watched all, if not most of these. To anyone living outside the U.K. every one of those murder who-dunnits is shown around the world. Last week I watched a programme showing how the Midsomer Murder programmes were made and learned this series is exported to 220 countries! Not a misprint 220 countries.

5

SEASONS TOYS AND GAMES

I learned very quickly that as in fashion toys have their seasons too. In Spring to meet the March winds adults and children rush to launch kites which come in a huge array of shapes, colours and sizes. As a child I marvelled at the skill some people showed, especially with the extra-large types that required two handed control. Then, with days of growing daylight toy sellers brought to the forefront playballs, fishing nets, skipping ropes, hula-hoops and other toys for outdoor activities. Unlike the calendar the world of toys has more seasons that move rapidly in and out of fashion.

Some, like seaside items and Halloween, automatically fall into place but somehow and I've never discovered how, children seem to instinctively know when the marble season and other outdoor games are about to begin. For girls hop-scotch has never gone out of fashion and all that is required is chalk and an empty shoe polish tin.

Seasonal toy trends in Britain and Ireland follow a similar pattern. There is one major exception and that is fireworks. Now, straight away someone is thinking; fireworks are not toys. Quite right, but in the 1970's many U.K. retailers sold them to young children and even in the 21st century youngsters still manage to purchase these items. In Ireland however, apart from the fact that Guy Fawkes and November 5th are not remembered in any shape or form fireworks have been banned from retail sale for as long as I can remember. Although Halloween is a hugely enjoyable party-time throughout the country, the few firework displays seen there are carefully organised or approved by state or semi-state bodies. As a result the Republic does not suffer the same rash of injuries as Britain.

One of my biggest seasonal sellers was the horror mask and of course the witch mask and conical hat. The masks came in three different sizes, the more horrific the better. On one weekend our Son Peter was assisting in Camberlys. During school holidays and half-term breaks he enjoyed the part-time working experience with my Father. A middle-aged man approached the counter and asked Peter “How much is the Frankenstein monster mask on the shop window model”? Without a moments delay and with a straight face Peter replied “One pound twenty-five, but you don't really need a mask”!
Fortunately the man had a good sense of humour. He bought the mask.

Every Halloween my Father created a Witch head and torso as a centre-piece for the window display. A cone hat, witch mask, black cape, it always captured the public's attention. One year a man enquired if the model was for sale. When told “only after Halloween”, he then asked if he could order a replica. Price didn't matter he said. We learned it was wanted as a present for a grandson. Happily Da produced another for the boy and then discovered the grandfather was Kevin McCrory, the Irish film producer and the man behind a couple of the James Bond films. He also held the American rights to a large segment of the Beatles music catalogue. Every year after that Mr McCrory placed an early order for his Halloween Witch. That is until my Father retired and the toy shop closed.

I think the earliest computer game during the 'seventies was something called 'Pong'. We had an 'Atari' console with two controls which our sons had great fun with, playing a game that was a cross between tennis and squash, batting a white bar across the screen. I still see this very same game around today in amusement arcades.

It was about this time that tougher safety laws for toys were put into effect. These laws followed the results of much research over the

previous ten years. Tests by the Great Ormond Street Hospital in the late 1960s established positive links between many toys and lead poisoning found in children. Their examinations on over a hundred hospitalised children found nearly half had higher lead levels in their blood than normal youngsters. As a result of the wide-scale publicity given to their report and that of other concerned groups adults became more careful with their purchases. This resulted in some customers expecting the impossible, such as a customer in Camberlys who showed interest in buying a 'Fisher Price' garage.
“Is this toy guaranteed to be unbreakable”?
My Father shook his head. “No, but I will guarantee that if it is treated roughly it will surely break”.
He smiled “Have you ever heard of an unbreakable toy? Left unsupervised, a child could demolish a safe”. An exaggeration but he made his point - and the sale - as a result of his being honest, I believe.

Writing of Fisher Price and quality, there is no doubting the high quality of their toys. Since their beginnings way back in 1931 they have produced over 5,000 different toy models. However, in 2007 there was a major lead scare with a few 'Dora the Explorer' and 'Sesame Street' designs. Over a million items were recalled. Other firms in recent times have had similar experiences and in the majority of cases the toys were 'Made in China'. Although China's toy industry has lagged behind in dealing with high lead levels and unsafe products most makers have improved their quality control methods.

Again on the subject of quality, a salesman who called regularly upon my Father showed him a rather cute looking mechanical chicken. It was about ten centimetres tall and when wound up, bent forward pecking on the counter top.
“Aby ... this is a great seller. I've sold hundreds ... you''ll shift loads of these”.

Da was amused at first, then, picking it up, he ran his finger across the beak. He gave the man a searching look. “Have you looked carefully at this? The beak is so sharp it would rip a child's hand in seconds”.
He was talking to someone who didn't want to know.
“I'm telling you ... I've sold hundreds of them ... look at the price tag”.
Da shook his head.
“And I'm telling you this toy is lethal. If they were free I wouldn't touch them and I'm surprised with all your experience in the toy game you're so damned reluctant to acknowledge how dangerous this is”.

The above incident reminds me of a wartime story that further illustrates the hustling mentality behind certain sales deals. During the war, on a Winter's night in London with 'black-out' regulations in force a four wheeled horse-drawn cart moves through the East-End. The driver hails a familiar figure and nips down off the heavily laden carriage. Sidling up to his acquaintance, he quietly mutters “Ere, Harry ... Interested in a real bargain, are ye?”
The other man's eyes light up. “Wotcha got”?
“Under the tarpaulin ... A consignment of sardines”. (An item unavailable during the war years).
“Ow much?”
“To you ... one thousand smackers. You'll double your money in no time”.
Deal completed and with goods transferred to a nearby warehouse the sardines are so in demand the whole shipment is sold over and over, soon reaching a value of several thousand pounds. At this stage the sardines are offered to a Covent Garden trader. As he thinks about the deal he opens a can of sardines to sample them.
“Phew” He utters in disgust, spitting out the mouthful. “They're rancid. Those sardines are so off ... they're poisonous”.

The seller scoffs. “What did you open the tin for? The sardines are not for eating. They're for buying and selling”!

With all the government promoted checks on toys, the greatest responsibility for ensuring safety standards are adhered to lies mainly with importers and retail stockists. A small number will evade regulated checks and so ultimately the final inspection sits on the shoulders of the toy purchaser. The responsibility for selling poorly produced or dangerous toys may lie elsewhere but discovering that after a bad purchase or injury won't ease matters. My observations have led me to believe that the majority of shoppers will carefully examine the labels on food and household goods but somehow there are some who pay scant attention to safety information on toys.

One game I returned to was football. Not as a player, my playing days ended in the early 'sixties, but as a coach to one of Dublin Maccabi's junior teams. Colin at this stage was a member of the club's gym and self-defence section and Peter was playing for the Junior under 14 football team. With Ian and Neal eager to play competitive football I suggested to the club that two more youth teams be formed for youngsters under eight and ten. I was prepared to coach the older section and a friend, Alan Ellison, volunteered to look after those under eight. In both cases we looked after these squads until the players reached sixteen and mature enough to play on the senior second eleven. For me, it was six great years coaching, and watching the development of my younger Sons and their pals. At the beginning of each season and with the boys getting taller I bought them a new set of jerseys, shorts and socks, one season all white and the following year blue. We never won any trophies or achieved higher than 4th position in the league but one year were unlucky to lose in a thrilling semi-final cup match. Yet every week through the season, in all kinds of weather, the boys turned out eager to play. For me the only disappointment was that most of the parents didn't bother to watch and support their lads. What the boys thought I don't know but I never got to understand the adults lack of interest.

1976 Junior Football Team
Roy Samuels
David Baker, Shidan Bismilla, Graham Walters, Harold Eppel, David Woolfson, Ian Samuels
Leonard Abrahamson, Gideon Taylor, Brian Stein, David Caplin, Graham Lawson,
Howard (Howie) Danker, Harold Lewis

It has been said that game play and sport can bring out the best and worst in people. Well I'm certainly not going to give an in-depth account or analysis of several personal studies or observations over a long period of time but I do believe that playing sport under proper tuition and guidance can help character building. What I have observed down the years is how some players, while playing with great determination and a desire to win, will play fairly and within the rules. Others, even among professionals and the most skilful amateurs resort to cheating or brawling. Fair or foul, on both counts, a close observer can learn much about two such people playing, for example, a game of tennis. Frequently in many sports, the foul play is neither subtle or concealed. Tempers flare, fists and boots lash out to be witnessed by the young and impressionable. Once, while watching a football match of under 10 year olds, two lads got into an argument. The incident began with jersey tugging and name calling and when one lad felt he needed to really impose his will on the other he took off a boot and began hitting his opponent over the head. The referee was on the far side of the pitch unable to nip things in the bud quickly. Being close to the scrap, I ran to intervene. Grabbing the boot I said to the offender "Sonny, this is a game ... not a battle."

I doubt if my words had any effect whatsoever. Young people see violent outbreaks of temper every week on television mainly on Football and Rugby sportscasts. If the big stars do it and in many cases get away with a pathetic warning, then, as I've said the young are set a bad example.

6

MOVING ON

Between 1976 and 1978 we celebrated with Family and friends our Sons; Peter and Ian's Barmitzvahs. With the experience of Colin's ceremony and receptions behind us we looked forward to both occasions in a more relaxed manner. Looking back I can still recall two confident relaxed teenagers, who like Colin before them appeared to clearly and precisely read their allotted Hebrew passages from the Torah, a portion from one of the five books of Moses. I used the word 'precisely' for in any reading from the Torah every single word must be exactly enunciated and clearly audible to the whole congregation.

With each Barmitzvah we arranged for a following luncheon and in the evening a catered house reception. In Dublin (unlike many towns) it was almost traditional for families to extend a Simcha (celebration) over an entire weekend, starting with a Friday night buffet for visitors from abroad or as the Dubs' called them 'out-of-towners'.

For most women, Anita's itinerary over that period would have been enough to get on with but as our youngest Son Neal joined his brothers in Wesley College she made time to go house hunting, again!

I remember the day well. It was a Friday. I'd no sooner sat down to dinner when Anita almost exploded with excitement. With a rush of words, she described in great detail a house that sounded too good to be true.

“I saw the most magnificent for-sale house today. It's a colonial styled building on a third of an acre, set in a cul-de-sac of five dwellings, all different designs. The hall is enormous, with a central staircase that splits half-way up to join a surrounding landing overlooking the hall. The lounge and dining area are on split levels 42 feet long (14 metres). Then the very large kitchen and breakfast room are also on split levels and there's a family room and ...."

At about this point I called a halt to the rapid sales pitch, for that is what it was. Anita was selling me a house.
"Alright ... it sounds fantastic, but it's too expensive".
"I haven't told you the price yet".
"You don't have to. If it is half as good as you've described it cannot be within our range".
Anita sailed on. "Make a guess at the price", she responded brightly.
Now I was becoming interested.
"Ifff this house is anything like you've described and at a price you believe we can afford, I'll be amazed".
"Guess? Guess how much?"
Anita knew she had aroused my interest, not greatly, but enough for her to work on. She pressed me for a response. Weighing up the description of this bargain colonial styled building, on a third of an acre, in a prime location, I tried to calculate two figures. Firstly, what such a place should be worth and secondly what her 'surprise' price could be.

"Alright ...I said, ... I'll play. Bearing in mind, I haven't seen your amazing dream house, the place should be worth somewhere around £80-90k (About £1m in 2008 values) and you're going to tell me the asking price is ... £70k"!
Anita smiled broadly. "We can buy it for 45 thou".
I couldn't believe the figure. "Anita ... your details and a price of £45,000 do not stack up".
"That's because the builder has a pressing cash-flow problem. He built a few special one-off designed houses and this last one, not

quite completed, was intended for himself and family. The bank manager is now leaning on him, keeps saying he can't afford the place. The man is desperate to make a cash sale fast and that explains the price. He cannot wait for someone to begin mortgage arrangements".

Next day, a Saturday, Anita and I went early to the building site. On a short rising drive the grey bricked house stood at the centre of a large plot of land. It was just as Anita well described, a most impressive building, about 80% completed. Within seconds I realised here was an opportunity to make a substantial profit. To Anita I said "You were spot-on, it's a fabulous place. My immediate thoughts are to clinch the deal as soon as possible and then in two years sell it".
"Sell it"! Anita couldn't believe what she was hearing.
"Yes. In two years we'll get several times the builder's asking price".

Straight away she realised we could in fact make a huge profit in quick time. When the builder came a short time later we assured him of our ability to complete a fast transaction. However, I reminded him that speedy legal searches and contract matters were not something we could guarantee, but we would have our solicitor draw up a suitable letter for his bank manager to say that, provided all the legal paperwork was in order, we would buy the house.

After 8 happy years in our home at Foxrock we found a buyer very quickly. So quickly we were reluctantly forced to move out and arrange a temporary letting whilst the new home was being completed. A four week delay stretched to 8 weeks and we rented a 4 bedroom terraced house in a new development at Kimmage in South Dublin. A four bedroom dwelling may sound like a spacious accommodation but this particular place was anything but that. Within hours our sons referred to it as 'The Lego House'. The only redeeming feature was that the house was minutes away from the

Dublin Maccabi Sports centre, where all the Family were actively involved.

The sequel to the 'Colonial' house purchase was, we did sell it two years and six months on at a very handsome profit.

Home number five was 29 Ardilea Downs, Roebuck. Another South County address. We could, from the upstairs windows see across Dublin Bay to the Swords headland and lighthouse jutting into the Irish Sea and with Bray Head in Wicklow facing, forming a perfect horse-shoe bay. Every evening before retiring to bed I took long minutes watching ships gliding in and out of the bay and further beyond see the 'planes on their approach into Dublin Airport. Number 29 was my favourite house.

My Family and friends discovered a long time ago how absent minded I am. So it came as no surprise for them to hear that on some work-day evenings, I headed home to the wrong address. On the other hand, I discovered that several friends sometimes went to visit us at a previously owned house. After other changes of address Ian's father-in-law, Gerry Lakmaker, said to me, “I'm getting wise to you. After many years of having you ruin my address book with your constant moves, different telephone numbers and so on, I now enter your details in PENCIL”!

In 1977 Charlie Chaplin died. To my Parents generation he was a comic genius, a giant of the cinema throughout the 1920s. Even in the 1930s and 1940s he made notable films such as Modern Times and The Great Dictator, a film ahead of its time and one of my early favourite pictures. Unfortunately in the early 1950s he was witch-hunted out of America because of alleged claims of Communist affiliations. Although he swore he would never return he did so in 1972 to receive a special Academy Award. Chaplin, who was born in

England, was knighted in 1975. Months after his funeral his coffin was stolen from a cemetery in Switzerland. It was believed this act was to extort money from the Chaplin family but never confirmed by anyone. Sometime during the Summer the coffin and remains were found near the town of Noville.

There comes a stage in family life when children decide the family holiday is no longer their scene. It's part of a natural strike for independence and like most loving and caring parents we were disappointed when our eldest sons, Colin and Peter, said they had other plans for the 1978 holiday. At the same time having been down that teenage road ourselves we understood their reasons. So it was that Summer, just Anita, Ian, Neal and I, travelled to Spain. It was flaming June, not the kind of weather Ian and Neal liked, so a lot of our time, when Anita lay baking under the sun, was spent in a beach bar watching Scotland, Britain's only football representative at the World Cup, lose to Peru, then draw with Iran. For their final qualifying game to enter the next round they needed a win over Holland by three goals. Even with Liverpool stars Kenny Dalglish, Graeme Souness and the talented Archie Gemmill this proved too big a task and at the end of an exciting match they could only get a 3-2 win. For the many Scottish supporters who crowded the bar it was a bitter let down. On football free periods we took boat sightseeing trips and saw some nearby towns but for Ian and Neal the constant heat sapped their interest. Like their senior siblings they began talking of other holiday options and from here on Anita and I would be making holiday plans for just the two of us.

When, after almost 18 years holidaying with our Sons we eventually found ourselves travelling without them it seemed quite strange. Time and time again I'd go to point out a place of unique interest to our boys, who were not there! I'll bet this has happened to other parents. We greatly missed the family drives to the South coast of

England. Afterwards we spent a few short breaks at Bournemouth including a couple with my parents. On our visits we always called to the Russell-Cotes Art Gallery & Museum. This unusual, must visit place, is on the East Cliff about three hundred metres from the pier. A fascinating building, it was built in 1901 to the order of Sir Merton Russell-Cotes for his wife's birthday. Sir Merton and Lady Russell-Cotes on their world travels assembled an amazing collection of art and these many items form the backbone of the Museum's display. The house, in its privately owned times, saw many distinguished guests at the turn of the 20th century, including the great Shakespearean Sir Henry Irving and other stage legends such as Ellen Terry and Sarah Bernhardt. Sir Russell-Cotes, a one time mayor of Bournemouth, in his will bequeathed the house (upon the death of his wife) to the Council, who appear to maintain and develop it well. Over the years the building has been extended with a larger art gallery, a café and children's play area.

A little add-on story to the above relating to one of our Museum trips. I think it was 1977 when we were dismayed to find several large hideous paintings displayed near the entrance hall. When we asked one of the staff about the new additions he mournfully told us they were backdrop paintings provided for the recently released film 'Valentino'. For several weeks the Museum was rented as the home of Rudolph Valentino, a big romantic star of the silent film era. The Italian/American actor variously called 'The Latin Lover' or 'The Great Lover' was worshipped by millions of women in the 1920s and his sudden death in 1927 aged 31 created a huge wave of grief.

We understood why the paintings were required to lend a more opulent look for the film based on his life but could not grasp why the enormous frames were still in place. Close up they did not look well painted or appealing. In reply to our critical views the assistant brightened up and said "The staff are unanimous in that we believe they are not compatible with the gallery's image. The governors won't listen, so we're gathering public opinions to get them removed". The man produced a clipboard with hundreds of names and critical comments to which we added ours. The staff's endeavours were rewarded. On our next call the Valentino paintings were gone.

By now my Brother Melvyn had long moved away from the Deli and Restaurant business, selling both within a short period. Having worked long and hard hours as one does in that line he, like myself, embarked upon a new trade. With Wife Avril, who spent many years in the retail antiques business, they opened an antique shop in the city centre. It was named M. Samuels and they quickly established a fine customer base. On top of this two important London dealers whom they met at trade fairs took a shine to both and helped them greatly with introductions to useful trade contacts.

On holiday in Portugal in 1977
Melvyn and Avril with daughters Fiona (left) and Michele

A house move came next when Melvyn, Avril, daughters Fiona and

Michele, moved to a lovely new new home on the Southern edge of County Dublin.

More Family changes took place. Colin completed his education at Wesley College and with top marks in every subject was ready to decide on the future. As he said at the time; "You asked me to produce good results and I have, the top marks. That's my desk work and cramming for exams over and finished".

He was right. Knowing he had a good brain I'd always encouraged him to study. Year on year Colin's results improved on an impressive rising scale. Now, after a hard grind he wanted to sit and discuss his future options. Having spent several school holiday breaks working at Cambie he became aware of our rather antiquated bookkeeping system. In the early days it did not present a pressing problem but as turnover increased rapidly a more modern accounting package needed to be installed. The situation was tailor-made for Colin to walk into. After careful consideration the Company purchased its first computer and in jig time Colin got to grips with it. Not only got to grips with it but managed to get more use out of the system than the suppliers believed possible. The sales manager was so impressed he asked permission to bring over one of his firm's directors to enquire of Colin how he managed to extract more functions from the software package than they could work out for themselves.

A very close friend of ours, Elaine Bloom, told us her sister Tamara had just undergone a thyroid operation. On top of that the young woman's marriage was not faring well and with two small daughters and mounting household debts Tamara, not surprisingly, was feeling low. I didn't really know the sister that well but as the hospital was close to the office decided to pay her a 'cheer-up' visit. With that in mind I prepared a thin cane with a hand coloured daffodil stuck on top. Held forward like a wand I marched into her hospital room and asked if she had a vase I could use for this newest and most tender variety of daffodil. She burst out laughing then, clutching her throat pleaded; “Please don't make me laugh, it hurts”.

Towards the end of my 15 minute visit Tamara asked if she could call upon me after a recuperative period. Curious as to why she wanted to see me, I said “yes”. With a fair sized family living nearby she wasn't short of people to talk to.

Two weeks after my hospital visit Tamara called to see me. Her husband, a man I knew in a casual sense appeared to be having business problems. The survivor of a Nazi concentration camp the man was prone to fits of depression, finding it difficult to manage his affairs, running the family into debt. With two daughters of school-going age Tamara was looking to augment the family coffers with a part-time job, hence her call, to seek advice on how she might go about finding such a position. In early opening probes it became clear she had little business experience that would help land her a job of any kind. Her assets as I saw it were, she seemed to have a quick mind, was a smart dresser and could speak well. In other words she presented herself well, one of the first requirements for a top salesperson. I told her so and suggested she try that avenue for employment. When she protested saying she had never sold anything before, I gave her a 30 minutes talk on how she might go about trying her hand at such a task. We chatted on for some time and it became clear she was too nervous to approach anyone for a job. Suddenly, she asked, “Would you be prepared to let me try selling for you, purely on a trial basis, with no commitment on your side”?

I wasn't looking to employ anyone and said so. However the idea of having someone else covering a portion of the sales ground appealed to me. My counter offer was this, “I'll pass over just a few small accounts for you to get started with, help give you a little confidence and a base you can add to. On payments we get you will receive a commission payable every Friday". Tamara seemed relieved, more than pleased with the opportunity and so began a sales career that lasted 10 years with Cambie.

Her sales figures improved quickly and in time she traded in her banger of a car for a new one and for the first time in years was able to afford holidays abroad. On the few Fridays her commission was low I saw to it that the figure was topped up to ensure she was not faced with a money problem.

The entire family was still very actively engaged with sports at the Dublin Maccabi & Carlisle centre. Anita, a regular member of the tennis section played several times a week as did our sister-in-law, Avril. Sons Colin, Peter, Ian, Neal were involved in at least one section, from football and tennis to martial-arts. Melvyn and I had both retired from playing football but he, an excellent rugby player was still kitting-out every week. At one stage Melvyn moved away to one of the premier Irish clubs Palmerston. There he got to play for their 1st team, a very notable achievement. On top of that he was a fine wicket-keeper and played for Carlisle's first eleven in the top division. Both he and I also began playing tennis. Pals, Sydney Bloom, Monty Ross, Aubrey Yodaiken and myself, played right through the year in every kind of weather. The no-hold battles between McEnroe and Borg, Sampras and Agassi, Nadal and Federer had nothing on us. Like Monty often said, "We left blood behind us on the court today"!

Once, in a keenly fought game between Aubrey and Monty the ball zinged from end to end, each player more determined not to lose than to win! At a crucial point of the match Aubrey pulled out his favourite winning shot a low forehand cross court smash. Somehow, Monty got his racquet to the ball and to his pleasant surprise, it flew back with Aubrey hopelessly stranded on the wrong side of the court. For moments he stood motionless, then, slowly approaching the net with hands on hips he called out, “Ross ... you are so ignorant. You are so ignorant, you didn't realise my shot was unplayable”!

We shouted, argued, and laughed a lot and Henry Solomon, a first team player observed, “I'm not too sure what your game is, but you're clearly having a whale of a time”! And we did, most Tuesday evenings under outdoor lights and Sunday mornings, with hardly a miss.

One day I received a call from Leslie Silverstone, a long standing club stalwart. “Roy, the club is going to celebrate it's 60th anniversary in the Autumn; 1919 /1979”.

Rather belatedly, they've asked if you and I could put together a commemorative magazine, similar to the one we did for the 16th (Scouts). It would mean collating info from each section and urging the committee to forward advertisements and lists of subscribing patrons in time for publication. I'm prepared to do it if you are”.

Now, for a second time, Leslie and I spent many hours tracing names, facts and figures. Our task covered the cricket, football, gym, rugby, tennis and table-tennis sections. The club proudly boasted an impressive number of Irish Internationals but sad to say, twenty years on, almost all Maccabi and Carlisle teams ceased to exist. After a total of about 90 years all that remains of a once thriving Dublin Maccabi & Carlisle sports club with the finest clubhouse and ground facilities in Ireland are the memories of those who participated and our magazine, a copy of which was given to the Dublin Jewish Museum.

The only known photograph of Roy and Melvyn together on a Maccabi team.

7

1980 - THE HEARTLESS EIGHTIES

That is how one commentator of the time described that decade. A time when people cared less about people and more about money. Others have claimed it was then, that the 'Materialistic Society' was born. Well ... yes and no to that general view. True, new legislation helped pave the way for a new breed of entrepreneurs eager to get rich quickly. This came about when Margaret Thatcher as leader of the Tory party gained power in 1979, becoming the first British woman Prime-Minister.

Sweeping away many restrictive practices, Thatcher 's policies opened the way to more competition. When some unions tried to oppose her plans they were quickly crushed by new laws enforced by police action. State monopolies were shaken by reduced support, personal benefits for the worse off reduced, while tax cuts were allowed for the better heeled. State assistance gave way to personal ambition and in some cases, greed. In her drive for a more open society 'greed' was not what she advocated with her radical changes. In fairness to her real aims I suppose it would be fair to say Margaret Thatcher's philosophy might be summed up with a remark she made during an interview, "No one would remember the Good Samaritan if he'd only had good intentions. He had money as well".

In writing of the 'get rich quick at any price' mentality of some people, I wonder how the same chroniclers of the 1980s who bandied the word 'greed' about with great abandon would compare their hoggish behaviour with that of the denounced bank speculators in 2008-2009.

In March a terrible disaster took place in the North Sea when a

'Phillips' oil platform capsized during a fierce storm. Nearby vessels rushed to the scene and plucked about ninety workers from the freezing waters. Sadly one hundred men drowned. The inquest never fully explained how the accident happened but some people alleged the oil company were in no rush to find out where the faults or responsibilities lay. Ironically 1980 was also the year Britain's oil exports exceeded imports for the first time.

Ten years into a Northern Ireland conflict that became known throughout Ireland as 'The Troubles' the extreme factions of Republican and Loyalist groups raised the tempo of violence. The incidents of shootings and bombings grew with tit-for-tat killings. At the height of terrorist attacks during the Summer of '79 the violence found its way into the Irish Republic. Earl Mountbatten of Burma, a frequent visitor to County Sligo was killed by the I.R.A. while on holiday with family. A bomb was placed on board his boat and detonated by remote radio control. Killed in the explosion with Mountbatten were his 15 year old grandson and a local boy, also 15. An elderly lady guest on board the launch died days later from her injuries. On the same day in Northern Ireland 18 British soldiers of the Parachute Regiment were killed when two massive bombs were exploded close by. This act was retaliation for 13 Catholics killed by the Regiment in 1972. Following the slaughter of soldiers a painted slogan appeared on a wall in Belfast. It read:

"13 gone not forgotten,
we got 18 and Mountbatten".

It was in the Spring of 1980 when Melvyn dropped in to see me for a morning tea as he did from time to time. On other days, I called upon him, same ritual tea and Kit-kats and a chat about Rugby, Football or Family. On this particular day he asked if I'd been near Powerscourt House recently. He was referring to a mansion just yards from one of Dublin's busiest shopping streets, Grafton street, in the town centre.

The imposing building, once the city home of Lord Powerscourt, had in recent years been used as a business headquarters. Now, according to Melvyn, the massive building which stood at the end of a commercial block of buildings with three separate street entrances had changed hands again. This time a Cork business man named Robin Power, whilst retaining the original fascias was about to develop the site into an upmarket shopping centre.

My Brother seemingly had, in passing the site, made enquiries and noted the 'phone numbers of the agents who were handling the retail lettings. “I thought the place might be of interest to either of us for an expansion into toys or antique jewellery”.

In fact he was only lukewarm on the notion of opening another shop for Avril and himself but with four Sons coming along thought I might see an opportunity to grow a retail division, something that would in his opinion strengthen the wholesale business at the same time.

The result of our conversation was that I decided to take two lettings in the new Powerscourt Shopping Centre. With no financial connection to my Parents shop but with their permission both units were to trade under the name Camberlys. I invited our good friend Jack Restan to have his display company design and fit out the shops. This they did to the highest levels of retail standards. From the Camberly logo, the colour scheme, flooring, shelving units, in fact everything, we left to our design friends. The end result gave us a distinctive and unique identity. Among the Family and staff the shops were referred to as 'The News Shop' - and the much larger shop as 'The Main Shop'.

The small news shop was mainly a newsagents, also selling greeting cards, sweets, chocolates and tobacco products. The main shop was on the line of a Borders or WH Smith outlet.

Ian and Linda (Moore) Russell
outside the just opened Camberly Shop in The Trocadero Centre, London

Two more city Camberlys outlets followed. A shop within the prestigious newly built Westbury Hotel and our largest shop at the adjacent Westbury Shopping Mall. The owner of these two developments, several other hotels and a large construction company was P.V. Doyle. Pascal Vincent Doyle, to give his full name, was one of Ireland's most successful business men and I'm pleased to say that from day one when we first met, he and his eldest son Michael were wonderful and friendly landlords. He was a suave popular gentleman and I stress the word gentleman. Once at a big charitable function when chatting to a Nun, Mr. Doyle came by and stopped to say hello to both of us. Anita joked about a small marble table he bid and bought for over £2000, saying “I was prepared to pay £200 for that”.

His response was “Well come and live with me and its yours”. Now that wee bit of light repartee in no way suggested that he was a flirt. As I've said he was to all who ever met him regarded as a gentleman. Later that evening the Nun told me that he donated many thousands of pounds to several good causes which her convent supported.

Around this period our second Son Peter joined the business team, soon to be followed by Ian. In addition with the extra shop openings we were fortunate to take on a young lady who in short time became one of our retail managers.

Linda Moore was a treasure. A lovely bright personality, efficient and keen, a great example to the other sales staff members. Nearly thirty years on we still keep in touch, as we do with Anna Butcher (above with Colin & Ian's children), fifty-five years since we first met!

With the start-up of our retail operations, we introduced staff training, insisting that all members were made aware of how important customer care and service was. Once the company was up and running Ian took most of the responsibility for hiring new staff and with Linda prepared newcomers on how to attend customers. To reinforce their message I added two further important points. Within a day or two of an assistant joining the team I made it my business to welcome them on board adding “Please be aware I do not pay your wages. The people who enter our shops do, provided they get good service. Never say to anyone - 'I don't know'. If, during your early training session you cannot answer a customer query then say, 'please give me a minute and I'll find out' or get another assistant to help".

The result of our initiation programme was impressive. In short time trainees got to know where most stock items were to be found and were able to assist with anyone searching for gift ideas. All staff members were kitted out in smart grey suits, white shirts and green satin bow ties. For male members the satin bow was replaced with a plain green tie. Everyone took pride not only in their work and personal appearance but also in the state of the shop, wherever they served.

The reason I've written the above paragraph is because I know most people reading this will think, 'but those shops standards are to be expected by every shopper'. The sad facts are that here in 2010 most people I know complain about poorly trained staff in the majority of retail outlets. Perhaps, with tough economic times ahead traders may get to think more about customer service.

Because our shops were city based and close to the Westbury Hotel many of our customers were well known celebrities. Off the cuff I remember Peter Ustinov, film producer Kevin McCrory and two lovely actresses I had the pleasure to meet; Angela Lansbury and Shirley Bassey. Many politicians, writers, screen and television stars came by most weeks and all staff members were instructed to observe an important rule; a smile of recognition was fine but not to ask for autographs. Frequently when visiting the shops I noticed well known people browsing through books in a relaxed manner without having staff staring at their every move.

By 1980 the wholesale and retail businesses came under more separated management control with Colin in charge of Cambie Wholesale and me heading the Camberlys retail company. I still went on exploratory trips to trade fairs to keep abreast of what changes and developments were taking place in the toy and gift industry. Soon Colin would also take on this responsibility. In the meantime I decided to visit the Nuremberg toy show. This is the largest toy fair in the world and I was told that to walk every aisle through the many halls (just once) adds up to three miles, a claim I would not argue with. You will notice I added the words just once. That's because at all trade fairs visitors are bound to re-trace their steps. In fact some regular buyers will tell you that if you reverse your journey around the halls one somehow gets a different view of the stands ... seeing things of interest that were missed earlier.

On our first trip to a German city Anita and I were surprised to find store attendants and the public in general most helpful. I suppose conditioned by what we had heard and read of Germans being cool towards the British we expected the natives to show some resentment towards us. It was quite the opposite. Time and again when we stopped someone for directions we found, without exception, everyone assisted, even in some cases going out of their way to put us on the right path. Trains and trams also impressed; spotlessly clean, they ran on time with fares reasonably priced. As for Nuremberg itself, despite heavy Allied war-time bombing much of the old city appeared to be unmarked. It was hard to believe this very same place was where Hitler's massive pre-war rallies took place. A place where many tens of thousands of people gathered to cheer on the fuhrer despite his racist messages of hate. That awful frightening association tied in with the infamous 'Nuremberg War Trials' still haunt the memories cells of several generations which probably explains why Anita and I were initially surprised by our first impressions of people and place.

I mentioned the enormous size of the Toy Fair and yet there were few places to eat and sit awhile. Every hall, about nine in all, had a food serving counter selling drinks and snacks, mainly sandwiches and hot dogs. The latter were large, typical long frankfurter rolls. Not to our taste, they were hugely popular. From memory, I think only one hall had a limited number of seats available. Because of this we made it our business to halt and show an interest in the displays of several booths hoping to be invited to sit and take a closer look at the products and enjoy a proffered glass of orange or lemonade. These brief respites were most welcome and I don't think we could have made the rounds without those breaks. Mind you, at a few halts we did get to actually place an order or two. More about some of our highly successful tie-ups later on.

One hall that probably drew most visitors was one devoted entirely to model railway products with layouts the size of a big home lounge. These measured anything up to six by twelve metres in size with perhaps eight trains running at the same time. The elaborate constructions with towns, villages, lit dwellings and townspeople were all to perfect scale. I discovered in chatting to demonstrators that many of the displays were of a permanent nature and stored away after the show to be modified and updated the following year. The majority of viewers were men and like me, had to be dragged away by their wives or female escorts!

Two of our first 'Exclusive' tie-ups for the wholesale division were with Dutch manufacturers Ambi nursery toys and King jigsaw puzzles. These acquisitions for Ireland gave us entry to more prestigious retail accounts and by 1982 we also had the Irish selling rights for the popular game Mastermind. Now we were accepted countrywide as a major supplier to the retail trade.

My Parents were not not doing so well at their retail shop. The Dublin Corporation decided on major pipe laying works, a big programme which entailed one side of the roadway being excavated to a depth of about eight feet, nearly two and a half metres. The pipes were colossal and ratepayers were warned the street would be affected for more than six months. This meant all buses and transport had to be diverted away from the road with pathways narrowed to accommodate safety barriers and workers. On behalf of my Folks I tried to get the rate billing reduced, to no avail. Even a strong appeal to my long time contact Mister Murphy in the department failed. Soon the once busy thoroughfare took on the appearance of an extended bomb site. Large retail stores like Dockrells, Maceys and long established specialist shops suffered as shoppers went elsewhere. For most it was the beginning of the end and even now twenty-five years later Aungier Street and South Great Georges Street have not recovered the lost retail trading pattern.

During the Summer Anita and I made a couple of London trips to visit her Father who was ill in Edgware hospital. The Doctors were not quite certain as to why his condition was slowly worsening. Aged 75 but with no established illness they could put a finger on, all the medics could tell us was that his body was weakening. Soon after our second trip we received a message to say we should should return straight away. Two days later Anita's Father passed away. In looking back I remember a gentle man with a ready smile and moderate in his behaviour and opinions. Jack was the eldest of four children and was born in Kerch, Russia. When he was weeks old his parents moved to London in 1913, the city where his brother Solomon and sisters Fay and Renee were born. The family name then was Yaverbaum. As an adult managing a clothing factory he found staff could not get their mouths around such a strange foreign name so when people began calling him Mister Y he changed his name by deed poll to Wye.

A sideline to the name Wye. Quite often, when Anita is asked about her nee name she replies “Wye”. Back comes the embarrassed response “I was just curious”.

Following on the heels of the North Sea oil-rig disaster the general news scene in 1980 continued through the year with reports of downbeat and sombre happenings. The United States decided to boycott the Moscow Olympics in protest at the Soviet Union's invasion of Afghanistan. Rhodesia became Zimbabwe and Robert Mugabe gained a clear electoral victory to become Prime Minister. What a ghastly result that turned out to be! In London, the SAS were forced to storm the Iranian embassy when two hostages were shot. In a spectacular raid, crashing through upstairs windows, the Special Air Service team killed five gunmen and released all remaining hostages. It was also the year John Lennon was shot dead outside his Manhattan apartment by a young man who claimed to be an admirer! With mass unemployment in Britain the highest in Europe, price rises leading to inflation of twenty per cent and a Prime Minister denounced by many economists, Margaret Thatcher said firmly, "The lady is not for turning".

Thatcher's hard-line policies were not going down well and a growing number of party members grew concerned at public unrest which lead to street fights and confrontations with the police in most inner city areas. In Liverpool, with 60% of the town's workers idle, riots broke out and in Toxteth fierce pitched fights lasted for two weeks. However, future battles with the mineworkers union and Argentina changed the tide of opinion. So despite her early and well reported unpopularity 'Maggie' went on to remain in power for another nine years!

My bright news memory of the year was Liverpool F.C. winning the football championship for the fourth time in five years!

8

THE PRINCE, PRINCESS, PAPARAZZI AND POPE.

The word 'paparazzi' was not a commonly used term in 1981. Like me, my rather yellowing dictionary of that time was not familiar with the word , nor did most people know who or what the paparazzi were, not until a young lady by the name of Diana Spencer began to capture the public and media's attention. Later we learned of the Italian description for photographers who took un-staged candid photos of the rich and famous, at whatever their pursuits were. Either as single camera spies or in hunting packs they plagued their targets without care or consideration.

My earliest recollections of Lady Di, as she was popularly called, was at our Camberlys shops when she appeared on the front covers of most weekly and monthly magazines. Within a short time of her being noticed keeping company with Prince Charles, Lady Diana Spencer became, in a sense, public property. It wasn't just that and the fact she was pretty, the demure twenty year old had the same magic way of posing attractively as actress Marilyn Monroe had done. Photographers said of Monroe 'the camera loved her'. I reckon the same might have been said of the highly photogenic Diana.

Whenever Lady Diana's image appeared on the cover of a magazine that particular issue sold out in days. The Irish public's interest in the Prince of Wales's girl friend was huge. This at a time when the IRA were seeking to draw attention to their political cause. With every delivery of a Di cover I smiled, thinking of the rapid sales to come. So popular was she, that on some weeks we had five or six fronting magazine pictures on our shop racks. When the date for the Royal wedding was announced more space was devoted to speculation on the bridal wedding gown, honeymoon destination, place of residence and whatever else the writers could dream up. By July it seemed like the whole world was ready to see the televised wedding of Prince Charles and Lady Diana Spencer. News of the bride's dress, designed by Elizabeth and David Emanuel with an eight metre train, was leaked ahead. It was the stuff of fairy-tales, the Prince and Princess about to go from Saint Paul's Cathedral into the sun and a future of blissful harmony!

The televised marriage ceremony was watched by hundreds of millions around the world but as for a later life of blissful togetherness, well sadly, we all know how the story ended. In truth the couple were not well matched. Diana although of aristocratic lineage was on a different plain to Charles. She was very much an outgoing individual, a bright spirited woman who loved the limelight, while Charles's nature was more serious, in pursuit of quieter interests and in doing so, as the next few years went by, inclined to share more and more of his time in the company of another woman.

Although the Royal wedding received much attention in Ireland many people would remember 1981 because of more upsetting events. The name Bobby Sands came to the fore when the young man stood as a candidate in a coming North of Ireland election. At the time he was serving a sentence for firearm crimes. Charged with a criminal offence Sands protested, claiming he should be charged as a political prisoner. I'm not sure about the finer points raised on both sides of this matter but his demand was turned down. At this, he went on hunger strike, joined soon after by young protester Francis Hughes. After sixty-six days on strike Bobby Sands died of starvation. His friend Hughes died a week later. In all ten men died while on hunger strike.

We are all familiar with the expression 'bad news travels fast' and in recent decades world events have been transmitted faster and faster. One hundred and fifty odd years ago when Britain and France fought Russia in what became known as the Crimean War battle news took many days to reach England and the desks of daily newspapers. For example the now well documented true story of what took place before, during and after the 'Charge Of The Light Brigade' at Balaclava only came to honest detailed light weeks after the happening. Early reports gave no hint of the terrible blunders and the huge loss of lives due to incompetent officers who had little real knowledge of tactical warfare. In contrast, news of the Argentinian invasion of the Falkland Islands in 1982 was reported within minutes.

The remoteness of the British territories about 13,000 km (8,000 miles) from Britain, did not affect the speed at which communications were transmitted. Twenty-seven years after the Falklands war it's hard to believe the conflict lasted over two months, but every day up to the minute reports were processed by TV, radio and newspaper editors for rapid updated bulletins. We got to see and hear what was happening far away in the Atlantic almost instantly. In one famous account an on the spot reporter described how he watched fighter planes heading to engage the enemy, saying how he counted them all taking off and counted them all returning.

Whereas in previous times BBC radio newscasts came every few hours now we were getting bulletins every hour and soon to receive dedicated channels with televised and radio 24 hour news reporting. Because bad news is more prominently reported than good the public are bombarded around the clock with stories of woe and misery. A personal gripe? Yes ... and one shared with many others.

One of the most publicised events of 1982 other than the Falkland's war was the visit of Pope John Paul II. In Britain and Ireland great excitement grew with the anticipation of the Papal visitor. When he arrived in Dublin to perform a Mass in the Phoenix Park over one million people attended and today a large cross marks the site. In business we sold tens of thousands of Papal flags and at the end I could not recollect how many in total.

Writing of totals, one sequel of the Irish visit caused amusement when it was discovered that hundreds of newly born boys were christened 'John Paul'. A few years later the streets of Dublin were echoing with shouts of 'John Paul, come here at once', and 'John Paul ... wait till I get me hands on ye'!

After Dublin the Pope went to the town of Drogheda and addressed another mighty crowd. At this venue, talking of the troubled violent situation in Northern Ireland then, he pleaded - “On my knees, I beseech you to end the conflict”.

I watched this on television on an early evening broadcast and finding it very moving admit to shedding a tear or two. Thirteen years of bombings and shootings had already caused the premature deaths of over two thousand lives. Even so, touched and impressed as I was, I felt his plea would go in vain ... and sadly it did fail. The killings went on for another 20 years until a peace deal was done. A peace that has lasted but a few years, for today as I write this piece the media are reporting news of a fresh round of shootings in Ulster resulting in three deaths. It seems some people not content to live in peace prefer to reside in a bog of continual hate and violence.

Into 1983 and I was advancing towards my 50th birthday. I've never thought much about age, mine or that of anyone else and still don't. There are times however when my path has crossed with an old acquaintance and been surprised at how well or poorly they've aged. Life is funny that way. Thin turns to stout, black hair turns slowly or quickly to grey, or baldness! And fitness sometimes turns to ... ?

From day one we learn to to eat, walk, talk, read, count, play, train, work, care, love, learn all manner of things but what nobody can prepare one for, is how differently the ageing process affects the body. For most of my friends, Anita and me, it has become something of a joke when asked "How are you?" to reply, "Well apart from the few parts that have dropped off, not doing too badly thank you".

Wonderful Friends
Rose Yodaiken, Anita, Ralph Morris, Sidney Bloom
Shirley Morris, Roy, Aubrey Yodaiken, Elaine Bloom

9

NINETEEN EIGHTY FOUR

At the mention of 1984 my mind, with probably that of many others, will immediately relate the year and number to the title of George Orwell's classic book which was first published in 1949. When the book first came out, soon followed by a television series, 1984 seemed a long way off and people speculated whether any of the writer's purely fictional storylines concerning life in a future Great Britain would compare with reality.

Here now as I write in 2009 it is sixty years since Orwell, following the success of Animal Farm, sat down and wrote of a totalitarian run state named Oceania (Great Britain). His tale traced the path and fortunes (or mostly misfortunes) of a civil servant William Smith. The reason I mention this hit novel is twofold. Firstly, my memoirs have now reached 1984 and before I draw on my personal recollections of that time I thought it might be interesting to see if his vision of a future place called Oceania bears any resemblance to Britain as I saw it six decades on.

Many people would have read Orwell's highly acclaimed and successful book and remember some of the spawned phrases, such as "Big Brother is watching you". (A line frequently voiced today): and words like "doublethink" and "newsspeak".

Did life in Britain get to mirror his Oceanania? Not in 1984 it didn't. The picture he presented of miserable times with censorship, elimination of private property rights, for the majority of people faced with lowering living standards and civil rights was happily wide of what many readers viewed as a portent of what was to come. But since 1984, well, sadly a different picture emerges as we are now watched far more closely than in the past with cameras all over the place and many individual and personal details deliberately or accidentally made available to all and sundry. Local councils pay citizens to snoop on their neighbours and their workers extract items from rubbish bins to learn more about residents. Telephone land lines are frequently tapped by state and semi-state bodies, usually on the pretext that these actions are required for security reasons. Added to this more and more people are now open to more and more bureaucratic red tape. Hundreds of new state and semi-state laws imposed on citizens through every level of society. We are told these measures have been enforced for our own good and protection. The schools, hospitals and medical profession, police, businesses have been saddled and burdened, so much so, willing workers are impeded from doing their proper work. Most of these imposed regulations have been put into effect by the Labour party. Many citizens in the United States complain about President Obama and his polices imposing more and more legislation, in other words, they say there is too much government. This criticism could be laid at the door of number 10 Downing Street. Unfortunately, a result of the many imposed restrictions has led to people becoming less willing to assist others for fear of being penalised.

Once upon a time people in Eastern Europe living under communistic regimes envied those living in Great Britain, wishing they had fewer restrictions and could live in a freer society, free of intrusions into their lives. This was best put by the American Thomas Jefferson, who said “The greatest danger to the people are criminals and the government”.

For decades, at political party conferences, Conservatives, Labourites, and Liberals promised to rid the country of unnecessary form-filling, rules and forms frequently referred to as 'gobbledegook'. We're still waiting.

Returning to Mr. Orwell, he did have some extreme views from time to time and was viewed as a racist by some. However, when the royalties poured in enough to secure him financially for life his strong leftish political views appeared to moderate! I wonder why?

Before he took to writing novels, George Orwell, real name Eric Arthur Blair was a young journalist with the Tribune. He died quite young (of tuberculosis in 1955) aged 52.

10

BRIDIE & ANGELA

Recently I came to realise how many people claim to have a guardian angel or spiritual guide, a sort of ethereal being. While I cannot lay claim to such a being I do have and rely on two characters who one day stepped from the doodle pages of my sketch pad and have accompanied me ever since.

Some time around 1984 I was fortunate to meet Bridie and Angela, two Dublin City women who from then on have passed on the benefit of their grounded views. I know they won't be offended if I describe them as mature spinsters, who see life in a commonsensical fashion and from time to time have come to my rescue with their sane analysis of the mushrooming gobbledegook I referred to in the previous chapter most of us face in everyday life.

By a stroke of good fortune both of these dear friends moved to Manchester shortly after our Family arrived and now live close by. Not for a moment would I ever be so indelicate as to enquire of their ages but just between you and me, I figure their heads are on the young side of elderly.

In so many ways Bridie and Angela have assisted me on personal matters, taking care of correspondence, greeting cards of one kind and another with a brief and gentle message to let the recipient know they are still in the minds and hearts of Anita and myself.

11

HAPPY DAYS, HORROR DAYS

Right through the 1980s Anita and I shared happy holidays with our friends. To the Mediterranean Islands of Tenerife and Gran Canaria we enjoyed several wonderful holidays with Elaine and Sydney Bloom also Shirley and Ralph Morris. Equipped with tennis racquets we, like 'Mad dogs and Englishmen' played out in the midday sun. In the balmy evenings we sat in open restaurants dining, chatting and laughing the hours away. On one particular night Sydney assured me the local brew was fairly mild. It was a fruit and wine based concoction, Sangria, I believe.

His so-called mild drink sent my head into space. When it came to leaving the table my legs wouldn't follow the rest of the party. This caused much merriment and if it wasn't for Elaine's assisting hands I'd probably still be there.

A visit to Israel was made most enjoyable when Aubrey and Rose Yodaiken took us on what can only be described as a guided tour of the country. The original plan was to attend the wedding of Debra Josephson, daughter of Michael and Marlene in Tel Aviv and 'do a wee bit of sight-seeing'. The 'Yods' as we and other buddies affectionately call them had other ideas. Both knew the country well and literally drove us North to South to West. We had an amazing time with them.

On a memorable journey to Jerusalem we not only did all that the tourists do but enjoyed the added advantage of having our own personal guides who filled in background details to every visited site. “Wait till you get to the Western (Wailing) Wall we were told. You'll be bound to shed a tear”.

When we arrived at the square overlooking the Wall, Anita and the Yods walked to see it close up while I stayed behind to take in the overall scene. Upon their return, Rose said, "You look very sad Roy ... seeing the Wall has an emotional effect on lots of people".

I assured her, that was not what affected me. Impressive as it undoubtedly is, it was the thought of the many lives lost in battle at this same place that affected me most.

An even more stirring site for me and I'm sure for millions of other visitors is the 'Yad Vashem Holocaust Memorial Museum'. Since our trip a new building has replaced the one we saw. The majority of those reading this will be familiar as we were with pictures of the death camps but the Museum provides the most graphic gallery of the terrible atrocities carried out by the Nazis.

Walking around the exhibition I gulped, trying not to cry and just about held my composure, until we came to an outside building at the end of the main complex. There, in a darkened circular hall, was a wall with a large etched map of Europe. The various countries marked in black showed the number of Jewish men, women and children who were taken from their homes to the death camps. On the ground in front of the display stood a solitary flame and facing this with his back to me was an old man, bent with age. He was quietly reciting 'Kaddish' a mourner's prayer, most probably for a family member or even several kinsfolk. With that my tear flood gates burst open.

I understand the new Museum includes a 'Hall of Names' ... a memorial to each and every Jew who perished in the Holocaust. There are also paged listings of short biographies containing 2,000,000 victims.

Here are the words from a found victim's letter:

"Remember only that I was innocent and
Just like you, mortal and on that day,
I, too, had a face marked by rage,
by pity and joy quite simply,
a human face.

Benjamin Fondana
Murdered at Auschwitz 1944

Last weekend friends invited Anita and me for lunch. At one stage we talked of people we knew who escaped from the clutches of the Nazis and certain death. Our hostess said - "Why is it that today, all these years after World War II and with all the evidence surrounding the Holocaust there are still people who deny what took place?"

I was immediately reminded of a line or two from an old film 'Tobruk'. The film plot tells of a Jewish commando unit under the command of a British and an American officer on a mission to divert attention away from an imminent Allied Army attack on Field Marshall Rommel's desert army.

The American, in an attempt to reach a better understanding with the stiff Jewish leader, comments "I've always believed there is a bit of Jew in everyone". To which the Jewish officer responds "Yes ... but there is also a bit of Nazi in some people".

Just when we get over the horrific reminders of one barbaric act, so another comes along. In the early hours of an October morning 1984 a bomb exploded at the Grand Hotel in Brighton. This was the chosen venue for the Conservative party's annual conference. Five people were killed and thirty or so injured. Prime Minister Thatcher escaped injury but the IRA in a chilling follow-up call claiming responsibility said “We were unlucky but remember, we have only to be lucky once. You will have to be lucky always”.

The police later traced the guests who stayed at the Grand before the explosion and in 1985 arrested Patrick Magee who was found guilty of planting the bomb. He was sentenced to a minimum of 35 years but released in 1999 as part of the 'Good Friday Agreement'.

Again in 1984, woman police officer Yvonne Fletcher was slain when a member of the Libyan Embassy staff sprayed a machine gun in the direction of a protest group. The British government asked to interview staff members but were refused with officials claiming diplomatic immunity.

On a wider national scale a major confrontation took place when the Government drew up plans to close uneconomic coal mines. Straight away Arthur Scargill, the union leader, without a ballot, called for an all out strike. In earlier years a similar battle took place with Tory leader Ted Heath. The government backed down, forced to face a general election which they lost. This time around Margaret Thatcher was prepared with big stockpiles of fuel and following months of violent street clashes between police and miners the pit men reluctantly went back to work. At their peak output the mines once employed 400,000 men. Today in 2010 the total is 3,500.

To end my reminiscences of '84, I'll close on a sporting note.

Though only one event at the Winter Olympics at Sarajevo stands out in my memory, it was one that every viewer will recall. Ice-skaters Jayne Torvill and Christopher Dean won the gold medal for ice-dancing. Anita and I sat rooted in our chairs as the couple brought the audience to their feet with their pulsating interpretation of Ravel's

Bolero. When they slid to a climatic stop the crowd roared their approval. The noise level was topped two minutes later when the nine judges each awarded them maximum points. They retired from competitive dancing in 1999. However only recently, in 2009, I again watched them in exhibition performances.

In sporting life what could beat the above success? That's a simple one to answer for me! It was Liverpool Football Club winning the League championship (for the third consecutive season) winning against Everton in the final of the Milk Cup and beating Roma in the final of the European Cup.

In contrast two awful footballing tragedies happened in early 1985. The first was when an old wooden stand at Bradford City's ground burnt down during a game killing 56 people. A fire, thought to have started behind the grandstand, broke through to where the fans stood, creating panic. The resulting inferno took just five minutes to complete its damage. The second disaster was at Heysel Stadium near Brussels in Belgium. It was the venue for the final of the European Cup between Liverpool and Italian champions Juventus. The organisers seemed to be unprepared for the event with too few police and stewards on duty. This became apparent before the game started when rival groups began taunting each other. In addition there was no closed-circuit television system to notice the segregating barriers were giving way as a group of Liverpool supporters pushed forward. When the Juventus followers retreated a wall collapsed and it was mostly these fans who lost their lives. As a result of this disaster, the European football association banned English clubs from the competition for nine years.

12

A 60th ANNIVERSARY FOR ... BIG BOYS

One of the biggest selling books in the English language is 'Scouting For Boys'. It was written in 1907 by the founder member of what became the largest youth movement in the world; Lord Robert Baden-Powell. 'B.P' as he became known was not only Chief Scout of the British movement which reached a total of three million members by 1929 but was also accepted as World Chief Scout Leader.

In 1975 the 16th Dublin Scout Troop to which I proudly belonged, celebrated its 50th anniversary, an event I've already covered in this book. Now, in 1985, my friend and one time Scoutmaster Leslie Silverstone predicted our Group leader Maurice (Morrie) Gordon would contact us, as he had done before, to help organise a celebratory gala dinner for the 60th anniversary ... and he did.

It has been said that many boys never grow to be men, they just become bigger boys! If that is true then its a pity Lord Baden-Powell (a prolific writer) never wrote a book titled 'Scouting For Men'! Or ... 'Scouting For Bigger Boys'. I say this because the majority of ex-scouts I've come in contact with down the years are still young boy scouts at heart. And that ... is a compliment to the movement and its leaders. One wee illustration of this happened in 1976 when a VAT tax inspector called to examine our business records. Soon after settling down in the office he spied a magazine on a nearby shelf. "I can't quite make out the heading from here but is that what I think it is ... a Scout journal of sorts"? I explained it was in fact a magazine to commemorate the 50th anniversary of the 16th Dublin Troop. His eyes lit up. "Your camp site in Powerscourt was at the top of Lime Avenue, with all those swanky log cabins". When I confirmed that was so he went on enthusiastically, "I was with the Dundrum Troop, beside the Dargle River, near Council Rock".

I knew it well. For the next hour we talked of nothing but our young scouting days and it was with great reluctance he eventually broke off to examine our paperwork. For the next year or so, until he moved abroad, the inspector called every so often to the Westbury shop on Saturdays and dragged me away for a coffee and chat. Our suddenly born friendship simply came from young kindred past experiences.

The youthful scouting bonds formed ... generally, no matter how many years in the past, never vanish and that fact was always evident when Leslie and I contacted the 'old boys' for whatever re-union was on the cards. So when we commenced our 60th anniversary campaign hunt we received a great response. To illustrate, here from a copy of the 'Diamond Magazine' is our 1985 Letter from the Editors:

"In 1975, Naomi Taylor, Leslie Silverstone and Roy Samuels sat around a table piled high with photographs spanning five decades and several meeting later, drunk with our own tales of characters, camps shows and parades, we eventually produced the Golden Jubilee Magazine. This was no small feat since we spent 55 minutes out of every hour reminiscing.

We had barely recovered (so it seemed) when Morrie Gordon phoned and said, "Hi there, we want another magazine for our 60th Diamond Jubilee". Was it really 10 years on?

Once again we set out on a sentimental journey and once again the response was excellent - especially from overseas. A mention of the 16th seemed to bring out a magical spark with our 'boys' across the seas and we are grateful for their contributions. To them and all our friends at home who helped with this effort we say 'Thank you'.

Throughout the magazine there is, as one would expect in such a production, many stories of yesteryear and we're proud and delighted to record these in bringing the records up-to-date highlighting the important influence the Scouting Brotherhood has had on all our members. Scouts and Scouters of the 16th can take pleasure in the fact that as part of a large worldwide movement we have played our part well and can face the future confidently".

The Diamond Jubilee Dinner was held at Terenure Synagogue hall with every available chair space filled. The guest of honour was the Irish Chief Scout Eoghan Lavelle, a frequent visitor to our camp site in Powerscourt. In mentioning the estate where tens of thousands of scouts camped over the years I'm saddened now to relate that the beautiful Powerscourt Demesne, in County Wicklow, approximately 7 miles by 2 miles wide, is no longer available to the Boy Scout Association. Once owned by Lord Powerscourt (one time Irish Chief Scout) it passed into other hands and people who were more commercially minded. The scouts were evicted and the familiar sight of uniformed young boys and girls enjoying outdoor scouting activities is just a fading memory. A while ago Anita and I were driving near Powerscourt and she asked if I was interested in visiting the old camp site, to which I replied, "No. I have very fond memories of the place and in my mind's eye always want to see it as it was". A well kept fenced site with well built fitted log cabins, probably the finest in Ireland. And ... if you think it's just me that sees those scouting days in rose tinted specs then here are just a few similarly expressed extracts from the many letters we received.

"Dear Maurice, I received your letter and by a remarkable coincidence, just 2 hours earlier was talking to a patient (a scouter) and told him how fortunate we were as children in Dublin to have Powerscourt and our campsites and our devoted Group Scout

Leader a real American! Who I remember singing 'Buddy can you spare a dime' around the camp fire.

How lucky we were to be 'deprived' of glue, crack, TV and other sophisticated gadgets children need the character to withstand".
Ivor Citron Cheshire."

"... there are so many marvellous memories of my 16th days if I could write, I'd write a book that's real Irish! The prestige and honour of being invited to join the Rover Scout Crew in their hut for a cup of cocoa, amazing my wife and children with my stories of adventure and discovery, that I could start a fire with some dry leaves and two boy scouts! Beautiful memories of Powerscourt come flooding back; campfires, night hikes, the streaking from the Rover's hut to the plantation by the many now respectable , doctors, dentists, solicitors, accountants, business men. One day I may blackmail them! ... Marvellous times ... never to be forgotten experiences, can honestly say they were the happiest days of my life".
Len Cohen Leeds."

"... So many memories ...
Powerscourt a weekend when I was invited to a midnight feast ...
Another weekend when we got everyone up at 2am telling them there was an eclipse (after having advanced their watches!)
The wonderful weekends in Powerscourt with the inevitable stew!!
The Huts, Creosote, Logging, Campfires, - where does one stop?
I enjoyed every moment ...
Thank you 16th".
Richard Stein Israel."

"I always remember Powerscourt ... smell of wood fires – billycans, spiders, tea, with a background of beautiful scenery".
Jessel Hazelton Reading."

"Powerscourt ...
I remember Ralph Morris saying he built the main hut with his bare hands, Aubrey Yodaiken allowing us young scouts to use the Rovers 'bog-house' as a special privilege! Roy Samuels and Sydney Bloom's culinary demonstration with baked beans!! Trying to light outdoor fires in the rain, the competitions and swelling pride when badges were distributed... and always Powerscourt. The list goes on, all unforgettable, for those memories I'd happily do it again. God bless you the 16th Dublin".
Stanley Feldman Toronto."

"... neither time nor distance has dimmed many memories, as member of the Fox Patrol, promising to do my duty to God and the King (and having this explained in Morrie Gordon's American accent!!) the scent of the pines in Powerscourt, meeting Sir Robert Baden-Powell at the world Jamboree in Hungary in 1933, could go on for years ..."
Ralph Seligman Nassau Bahamas."

"It is not sentiment when I say that the 16th was a major influence on my early life, the fond memories of scouting life and Powerscourt camping weekends".
Brian Citron Middlesex."

On a personal level I learned how to fend for myself away from home, the rudiments of baking and cooking over a fire prepared from dry leaves and twigs. How to handle a hand axe with all the safety rules and later, a felling axe and cross-cut saw. Not as easy as it looks. Repairing campsite fencing and replacing split-bark panels in the huts. The importance of hygiene in the wild. Learning about trees and respecting wildlife. All of this and the fun shared with brother scouts, hiking, enjoying the campfires and convivial banter. Years ago, it was decided that scouts should no longer wear sheath knives and so I imagine they would not be permitted to handle hand or felling axes. I was stunned to read this week (here in 2009) that in a scout jamboree last Summer, at County Kildare, Ireland, camp fires were banned on the grounds of safety. Where on earth are the so-called liberal do-gooders, the green party and left wingers taking us? In all my many years associated with the scout movement I do not remember a scout reported for stabbing anyone. Yet now with all the 'safety' laws we have place stabbings take place every day and members of the above pressure groups often resort to violence and law breaking in order to achieve their aims.

Along with my Brother Melvyn most of my close friends were scouts: a host of young 'uns, some happily still around today. Their names pop easily into my head; Abe Baker, Zally Barnett, Sydney Bloom, Milton Jeffries, Joseph Levy, Willy Malkinson, Ralph Morris, Monty Ross, Dave Solomons and Aubrey Yodaiken. They too have added their grateful thanks to the wonderful 16th.

Believe me when I say the above selection of snippets from ex-scouts is only a fraction of the overwhelming feedback we received from our initial anniversary contacts. Again and again the fondly expressed memories underline how important the 16th Scout Group and its excellent leaders were to the members and of course the outdoor times spent at Powerscourt. Thousands of young boys reaped great benefits from learning how to fend for themselves, gaining knowledge, skills and confidence and though some might say there are alternative camping places near Dublin there is nothing to compare with Powerscourt. So ... the wealth seekers, the accountants, the golfers, the selfish adults, who could not accommodate boy and girl scouts on that wonderful estate can have the whole area to themselves, unhindered by the sight of young people gaining the same memorable experiences earlier generations enjoyed.

To tie in with the celebratory 60th Anniversary Dinner Monty Ross, as he did on the 50th event, proposed we arrange for a form of presentation to be made in recognition of Morrie Gordon's huge contribution of service to the 16th Dublin Scout Troop and scouting in general. I was not going to be the provider with another oil painting and said we needed something different. My alternative suggestion was for us to raise funds for a small plantation of trees in a local forestry area. The idea went down well so I contacted an official at the Dublin County Council and asked if we could make such a contribution. He was taken completely by surprise but after I mentioned a figure we had in mind he readily agreed. Not only did the Council designate a fair sized area for our project but they also to our great pleasure, placed a large 4 metre rounded rock with a copper plaque to commemorate Maurice Gordon's name and achievements at the entrance to one side of the plantation.

The whole presentation plan was a well kept secret right up until one special evening when Morrie was told by his wife of the Scouts wishing to honour him at a park on the South side of Dublin. When he arrived there was a guard of honour along with the older brigade lined up in front of the rock, covered with a white sheet. After a short address the scoutmaster invited him to unveil what proved to be a total surprise. He was so overwhelmed by the tribute and could barely stutter his thanks. Later we 'old boys' learned thereafter he paid frequent visits to the Dublin Council park showing family, friends and visitors the honour bestowed upon him.

13

LESLIE

Of the many people I have met, one man who had a large and long influence in my life was Leslie Silverstone. I first encountered Scoutmaster Silverstone at the end of August 1944 when I joined the 16th Dublin Scout Troop.

In Book One 'Sailing Through Plate Glass Doors' I wrote fully about my scouting days or as Leslie frequently referred them as 'scouting daze'. This now, is my story of and a tribute to a remarkable man.

Leslie, born in Glasgow in 1923, was the second of five children, four boys and a girl. Living in poor circumstances the family moved to Dublin and after a stay of five years went on to settle in London.

When he had completed his schooling days at the age of sixteen, Leslie's widowed mother thought he might stand a better chance of earning a living in Dublin, under the watchful eye of her married brother. Her well meant thoughts were not shared by his Uncle's wife who looked upon the youth as a house servant.

Working full-time as a 'gofor' in a wholesale fruit and vegetable market business he not only paid for his keep but was expected at the house to mow the lawn, polish shoes, run errands and carry out whatever chores were demanded of him.

Leslie's working conditions were tough. Over long hours in a bleak warehouse he hauled heavy sacks and crates of fruit and vegetables, at the same time keeping a check on all incoming and outgoing stock. He was physically and mentally strong, eager to take responsibility and over a few years one of the firm's senior directors took notice of his impressive performance and saw to his being promoted and financially rewarded.

In time he met and married a young attractive woman named Sybil Fox and they raised five well educated and well adjusted children. The youngsters must have enjoyed a great childhood and I say this because of my wonderful scouting days and experiences under his guidance. Leslie instinctively knew what made kids tick. Proud of our uniform and troop, we learned to appreciate the benefits of discipline, drill, competition, alongside team sports and games. With him at the helm, there was always a spirit of fun and adventure in our weekly programmes, whether at hall meetings or camping under canvas. To my knowledge there wasn't a boy who didn't look forward to Wednesday night meetings, Sunday outings, weekends or Summer camps.

Another side of Leslie lay in his passion for sports. Just as he had done in scouting, rising from the ranks to the position of scoutmaster, he captained the 1sts in rugby, tennis and football at the Dublin Maccabi sports club (formerly Carlisle). Here again, he led not only by example in fitness and skill but also in his approach to how the game should be played. Not in a dour, win at any cost manner but by way of applying one's best efforts towards the game. Win or lose his philosophy was if a player gave of his best there was pleasure and satisfaction to be gained either way. Here at this point I'll relate a humorous tale of Leslie's final game of football.

At the age of 44 there were fewer football players fitter that Leslie and at training or in the dressing room he would proudly state his intention of playing well into his fifties. Therefore it came as something of a major surprise when after a match he announced as he left the dressing room “By the way lads - that was my last game”. Several people tried, unsuccessfully, to find the reason for the sudden announcement. Eventually, it became evident Leslie was not interested in talking about the subject.

Six months later, our paths crossed and after updating our news and views, I slipped in the question, “Why did you suddenly quit playing football”?
He laughed. “Did you see my final game”?
“No ... I replied - Was it a stinker”?
Leslie laughed again. “Actually, I thought it was one of my best performances”. Now I was really puzzled and intrigued. “So what the hell made you decide to stop playing”? My friend drew a deep breath and began his story.

“It was a fast game. They had some players who could really run but we managed to hold them and reach half-time, level at one goal each. Straight after the restart we went into the lead and five minutes later they equalised. It was like a cup tie, end to end football. Then, ten minutes from the end, one of their players cleared his goal line with a high punt into our half. Their striker and myself ran hard for the ball. It was a fifty-fifty situation and we both went at it full pelt, neither prepared to give way”. Leslie smacked his hands together and smiled. “What a collision. We both fell heavily to the ground ... my whole body shook with the impact”.

“And that's what decided you ... to give up”?
He snorted at the suggestion. “What! because of a heavy crash? I've suffered much worse at rugby”. “Well, what then”?

“Like I said ... we both fell, head over arse. True, I felt a bit shattered but that did not cause the hurt. That came when the other player leapt to his feet, bent over me and said anxiously 'Are you alright SIR'”?

Leslie burst out laughing, for the umpteenth time and spread his hands wide. “In that one-liner Roy that young lad summed it up for me it was time for 'SIR' to retire”.

For another ten years or so Leslie continued to keep himself fit playing tennis. He'd won the club's championships several times; singles, doubles and mixed doubles. To stretch himself further he took up a new pastime, joining the Edmonstown golf club where he became President.

At this time Leslie was now managing director of W. H. Lamb, Fruit Wholesalers, the place where he started working as a messenger boy. He was also president of the Fruit Trades Association of Ireland Golfing Society. In that capacity and known for his good sense of humour and anecdotes he was frequently called upon to speak at golf functions. Some of these he committed to paper for the amusement of family and close friends. For me two things stand out in his writings - an ability to have fun with words and from real life observations, produce a tender insight into nature and human behaviour. Here is just a small selection of his verbal sketches.

YOUNG LOVE
Their paths of life had different ways progressed
Thro' many a year of toil they pressed.
Thrown together in their middle age by fate,
Thinking their chance of love had come too late.
There in the twilight they did sit,
Back o'er the years their minds did flit.
He touched her cheek, how soft her skin,
The darkness held a world within.
Behold, how young hearts did grow,
As passion thro' their veins did flow.
For youth was still upon their lips,
And love was in their finger tips.

AUSSIE DINNER
George said it was fair dinkum
When we sat down to dine
The food was so delicious
Also ... was the wine.
We all tucked in ... was lovely,
The 'taters and the meat.
Our hunger was no longer
When we got thro the sweet.
George said it was fair dinkum
Much to my surprise
'Cos I thought we were eating
Steak and potato pies.

Before I set out the last piece let me first print out the words of 'TAPS' sung to the military tune you have heard buglers play many, many times. These words delivered by Leslie hundreds of times at the closing of a scout meeting must have resonated through his mind before setting pen to paper.

TAPS
Gone the sun,
From the sea,
From the hills,
From the sky.
All is well,
Safely rest,
God is nigh.

Troop ...
May the Great Scoutmaster
of all scouts ... Watch over us until we meet again.
Troop ... Dismiss.

So here now is Leslie's version, or rather his interpretation of the above by way of a tribute to any scoutmaster who may have performed as he had done over the years.

In a way, although he never meant this as referring to himself, I think it most appropriate to introduce it here as reflecting the qualities of the man and friend I knew.

DAY IS DONE GONE THE SUN
A tribute to a scoutmaster

Did ever a man live like him.
A gentleman quite unique
Everyone was his brotherhood
Only good he could speak.

Did ever a man live like him
Family love he showed with pride,
He gave no one his favour
All men stood side by side.

Did ever a man live like him
Mixing with youth were his joys,
He gave his all to scouting,
Each generation were his boys.

Did ever a man die like him
His memory we cherish and adore,
The Great Scoutmaster he called to -
"watch over us"
Will watch over him, forevermore.

14

WHOLESALE CHANGES

The Concise Oxford Dictionary defines the word 'wholesale' in several ways -
'Selling large quantities (to be retailed by others)'.
'Changes on a large scale'.
'Far reaching wide ranging'.

In 1986 all of the above could be aptly applied to the wholesale company Cambie. In the wholesale division big changes were taking place.

On one of our Nuremberg Toy Fair trips I spied among a display of 'plush' (soft toy) items a furry orange cat. It was Garfield and it came in a wide selection of sizes and poses. Back then the cartoon character was hardly known in Ireland. Chatting to the chief salesman of the British distribution company I discovered their annual sales into Ireland were less than four thousand pounds. Immediately I requested the exclusive selling rights for Ireland, promising we could sell huge quantities.

Returning to Dublin, I excitedly showed a sample Garfield to the team. Saleswoman Tamara was not too impressed. “Does it come in colours other than orange”?, she asked. I was flummoxed and irritated telling her so. “You obviously are not familiar with the character, an orange cat that is GARFIELD”!

She shrugged. “Well if you say so ... I'll show it to the buyers and see what they think”. She did and we couldn't keep up with the demand. Time and again, Tamara complained, “Why don't you import bigger quantities”?

Our next purchasing coup turned out in time to lead to much bigger changes for the future. The new development began in a modest fashion. Colin and I visited New York's major gift fair at the Javits Centre. Nearing the end of what was turning out to be a fruitless search for new ideas Colin stopped at a small booth. Sitting behind a modest sized display of boxed cassettes, the salesman, unlike many brash New York reps, quietly introduced himself. Gary Pike, the Sales director of the 'Great American Audio Company' gave us a reserved sales pitch explaining that his firm produced just eighteen boxed twin-pack cassettes. Six of these sets contained music for relaxation and the other twelve; the soothing voice of the well known American psychologist Doctor Lee Pulos, giving advice, for example on -

'Learn to relax'
'Stop smoking'
'Build self confidence'
'Lose weight'
'Attain your goals'
'Relieve stress and anxiety'

On the strength of Colin's keen interest in the product we tied up an exclusive deal placing a decent sized order. The moment he showed the product to Peter his eyes lit up. “We're on to a winner here”, he said enthusiastically.

The immediate response boosted Colin's opinion and my confidence and as this story continues it will become clear how much the future development of our Sons' business ventures owed to that diversion into audio product.

The audio range sold reasonably well and more importantly it helped to open more new accounts such as Waterstones and Dillons. It was the beginning of our move away from the toy trade.

Yet another new addition to the wholesale business was a humorous line of plastic signs designed for home or workplace. Signs that read:
"You don't have to be crazy to work here, but it helps".
"Your mother doesn't work here, so tidy up after yourself".
"If I wanted it tomorrow I'd ask for it tomorrow".
"I love my job ... I need the $$$$$$$$$$$$$$$$$".

The slogans were available as wall plaques, in three sizes or as desk top signs. The American supplier was H & L Plastics, based near San Diego and owned by a man named Harold Lorsch. He was eight years older than me, medium build in height and girth, with a rather crumpled appearance. Anita, Colin and I met him at one of the Javits' trade shows in New York and struck up an immediate liking for one another. A tough but fair business negotiator, we found him to be a warm individual. On a holiday trip to San Diego he and wife Lynn proved to be admirable hosts, showing us most of the sights. The following year, after his wife passed away, he enquired what our coming holiday plans were. I explained Anita was joining Colin and Gayle on a vacation to Israel.
"And you"? he asked.
"I haven't decided yet".
"Well Roy ... I'll decide for you. You're coming to stay with me".
I tried to protest, saying it would create extra work for him and so on but he wouldn't take no for an answer.
"I'm feeling low at the moment and I need someone to stay here ... sort of break the silence and give me reasons to go out and about again. As for the extra work bit ... I have a nice Mexican lady who comes in every morning to straighten things out".

I could not refuse and must say my ten day stay with Harold was something we both enjoyed immensely.

If you ever watched the film or television series "The Odd Couple" then you'll understand what I mean when I describe our time together with that description.

While Harold was not as sloppy as the character 'Oscar' he was untidy and almost unconsciously, I found myself tidying up (like Felix in the film) after him. It soon became obvious and the more we went on in this way the funnier it became with him and me acting as it were, to a script.

To get a mental image of the San Diego bungalow where Harold lived, just cast your mind to any of those Hollywood films or glamorous TV plays, where the action was set in a wealthy location. His home, or 'spread' was perched on one of the many hills, overlooking a valley. To the rear ... the inevitable swimming pool backed with an orchard of oranges and lemons and without meaning to boast he described his home as "A modest property". When I chided him on this description he responded earnestly, "You should see where some of the millionaires live, on the next hill top".
I laughed. "Harold, who are you talking about? You ... are a millionaire ... probably several time over". He nodded. "Yes ... but these are multi-millionaires".

I suppose like many people are inclined to do in life, his observation was relative to how he measured his standing against the nearby neighbours.

To give you another glimpse of how he attained and later viewed wealth, I must first stress that Harold Lorsch came from a poor background. Born in Berlin, his parents and himself, (Jews) were forced to flee Germany in 1934, emigrating to New York. Harold, his original name Hans, was just nine years old. When the USA entered World War Two he enlisted at the age of 18 in the marines and fought at Bataan and Guadalcanal on the Pacific front. Returning to New York in 1945 he got a job stacking shelves in a supermarket. In that way he got to meet some of the salesmen who called to update their display stands. One friendly caller who supplied humorous signs and novelties announced one day that he was about to retire. Harold was quick to enquire if he might be interested in selling him his business. The man, a wealthy individual, was so taken by Harold's assistance and pleasant manner over his years of calling agreed not only to sell him the factory at a keen price but also offered him an easy payment plan with no interest to pay. In short time and working long hours the new young owner began raking up handsome profits. Around this time he met and fell in love with a pretty nurse, named Lynn. Anita and I met her many years on and thought she was one of the sweetest women we ever met. After their wedding Lynn joined in working for what became widely known as H&L Signs. From there on they never looked back financially.

A thrifty adult, Harold, when it came to others was a generous man. One morning he announced we were going to a large well known shopping area called 'The Valley'. In this place were located all the well established American fashion houses, such as Nieman Marcus, Bloomingdales and so on. Knowing of my past connection with the fashion trade Harold wanted me to assist him select a dress for his daughter Carol, a tall pretty blonde in her early thirties. The sales were on everywhere so I expected we could find a good bargain. About an hour into our search at Nieman Marcus I came across a beautiful red dress in her size. It was a sleeveless, sheath styled item with a wide gold belt.

As I removed it from the rack, Harold, looking keenly on, asked, “What do you think”? I checked the price ticket. The dress had been marked down by 25% and although I thought it nice, it still seemed expensive. “Wow ... it's $990.00”.

He brushed my remark aside. “Forget the price. Will it look well on her”?

“Fantastic - the colouring is just right ... she would look stunning in this. But Harold, $990.00”! He took the dress from me and hailed a sales assistant.

“Roy please ... stop with the price talk. If you're satisfied it's right for her ... I'm happy to buy it”. The purchase didn't end there. The senior sales woman placed the dress on a counter and enquired, “Would you also like the gold belt”?

I became more upset. “Surely the price includes the belt”?
“Oh no sir. The belt is $180.00”.

Before I could utter another protest Harold quickly replied, “I'll take it”. It didn't end there either. “And would you like it gift wrapped”? With that, I couldn't help myself. “What! ... A thousand dollar sale and you're going to charge for gift wrapping”? She thought for a moment but didn't answer me directly. Instead, she turned to Harold and smiling sweetly, said, “We'll gift wrap it free sir”. He smiled back and thanked her profusely.

Outside the store. Harold positively beamed with satisfaction. “Yep, I can see Carol looking swell in this dress”.
“Is it a birthday gift”? I asked.
“No. Although we're not religious, we always acknowledge the high holy days and festivals. This little number is a 'Hannuka' gift, (Festival of Lights)”. In Britain and Ireland, we pronounce the Jewish festival as 'Chanuka'. An eight day celebration period that usually coincides with Christmas.

“Well, I'm confident Carol will be quite pleased with her Chanuka

present". I said.
Harold laughed. "This is only part of her present. Each year I give her and Robert (his son) a cheque for $10,000". My jaw must have visibly dropped.

He laughed again. "You see, although Carol loves getting her 'Hannuka Gelt' (money), she still expects a boxed surprise present"

Another example of the man's generosity. Most evenings Harold and I dined out. He knew all the best eating places and was familiar to most head waiters. Time after time he managed to settle the bill before I discovered what he'd done. I realised after a few nights, he arranged somehow with the waiter's collusion to pay for the meals before I could act. Once I realised what he was up to, I demanded on our next evening out "Harold, you have got to allow me to pay - I can't even get my hand near my pocket". He grudgingly agreed.

We shared many wonderful days together, like a visit to the San Diego Zoo, one of the World's finest with many acres of land for animals to roam. Then a drive into the wooded hills to a town called 'Julian' and on another day a coastal journey taking in the famous bay bridge that leads to the impressive, huge 'Peace Bell', a present from the Japanese government. On our return we had afternoon tea at the Hotel del Coronado. The five star beach-side hotel, the setting for the Oscar winning film Some Like it Hot, with Jack Lemmon, Tony Curtis and Marilyn Monroe.

When the time came for me to head home Harold saw me to the airport departure gate. We stood there for a minute, unable to say 'goodbye'. He stepped forward and with tears welling up, we hugged for seconds. It was very emotional.

15

WIND UP TOYS AND WIND DOWN

In the previous chapter I wrote of how our wholesale business was moving away from the wholesale side of selling toys. Hand-held electronic, or computer games for children had not yet entered the general toy market. Yet we could see and sense changes were taking place. With children developing more quickly, girls and boys were giving up on certain toys at an earlier age. A widening selection of children's television programmes affected their playtime activities and in many cases also affected what mothers and fathers bought or were instructed to buy! Boys aged between 8 and 10 were less inclined to shove toy cars along the floor and girls of the same age group less interested in dolls houses and prams, especially since Mums were not buying traditional prams any more. Yes, there was 'Barbie' but Barbie was more grown up and glamorous than the nappy clad, crying, bottle fed, baby dolls.

My Parents' retail toy shop was showing signs of the general downward shift in buying patterns. In addition the street on which they traded had not recovered from earlier major road work upheavals. With dropping sale figures it seemed that sooner or later they would be faced with hard decisions, made harder by knowing how wonderful a business it once was. My Mother, now in her seventies, was also feeling the strain of working and though Da never complained about his active working schedule, I thought it best to help them deal with the closing of an era. I appreciated that my Father would miss chatting with customers and the business of business but at the same time, being a realist, would face facts. The only major problem was the shop lease still had another six or seven years to run and we were faced with the question as to whether the landlord would be open to a deal and perhaps accept a lump sum equal to half the outstanding periods' rent.

Not wishing to involve my Folks in any tense negotiations I arranged to meet the landlord in Bewleys café on South Great Georges Street or as most Dubliners called it “Georges Street”. We met in the morning, the landlord, his son aged about 20 and myself. With pleasantries exchanged and coffees on the table I laid out my cards openly. We had known each other, on good terms, for over 21 years, so I was confident of reaching a reasonable settlement. What I did not anticipate was the son either being present or pushing himself forward into the discussion. We had barely begun when he stopped me in mid sentence.

“Listen, we have you over a barrel, so there's nothing to discuss. You pay the full amount of what is due on the lease and that is that.” I was taken aback by the aggressive interruption and looked towards the father who sat silent for a minute, his face turning red. There was an embarrassing silence as I waited for him to speak. Slowly he stammered out a few words, saying that there was a legal lease in place and part way through his mutterings the son once again jumped in addressing me with his obviously rehearsed attack line.
“We have you over a barrel ...”
At this point, I halted him in full flow.
“First of all, this meeting was supposed to be between your father and me but as you're here and more than keen to have an input into our discussion, allow me to say something without interruption. I don't know how old you are, neither do I care. I hope you live to be a hundred and twenty and in the meantime, learn that life and business are not about putting people over barrels.

Before he could respond, I turned to the father and realising he must have been party to the son's planned bullish attitude and would not be open to anything less than a full settlement, indicated as pleasantly as

I could, probably through gritted teeth, that upon a provided statement for the full amount I would arrange a payment by return with the surrendered lease.

The only glimmer of satisfaction I gained from the encounter came months later. It seems the son convinced his father that now they were in possession of the shop he could turn it into a profitable business selling tools. It did not occur to them that the street no longer attracted shoppers and so the heavily stocked shop, with products imported directly from the Far East, failed big time.

Not wishing to tell my Parents about the outcome of the meeting and knowing of their financial situation, I settled not only the substantial rental bill but whatever Corporation rates were due. It would have upset them greatly to learn their cherished toy business ended in a sad financial state. What I failed to mention in book 2, was that when my Parents took possession of the shop, Da built every single shelf and display unit himself, including a large greeting card section and large centre floor counter for plush items teddy bears and the like. All of this huge effort in a big shop, at the age of 62!! A remarkable achievement.

For my Folks it was the end of a wonderful 20 year venture, one in particular Da enjoyed immensely. In an earlier chapter I wrote of young boys growing into not men but 'older boys'. I am convinced no other 'old boy' had as much fun with a toy shop as Da did.

16

ILL WINDS, FAIR WINDS

On a bright end-of-April morning in 1986 and as I headed towards the car for the office, I noticed an acrid smell in the air. As I looked around wondering if there was a local reason for this, my eyes began to smart. Within a day or two the media were getting increasing reports of a major nuclear accident in the Soviet Republic of Ukraine. The site was Chernobyl. Outside the Soviet Empire the name was virtually unknown and despite the political leaders attempts to keep the lid on the disaster, the most serious accidental nuclear explosion ever, Mother Nature forced them into confirming a critical nuclear accident had taken place.

Westerly winds wafted a radioactive cloud across Europe and in early May, after heavy rainfalls in Britain and Ireland, land samples were found to contain radioactive caesium. The samples came from a wide area; Northern and Western Ireland, the Isle of Man, Southern Scotland, Cumbria and North Wales. So as not to cause panic the British and Irish governments did not release all this information at once. But as the full facts came to light the authorities insisted that no damage to human health occurred. Recently, more than 20 years later a few hundred Scottish and Welsh farmers were still coming across lambs affected by soil radiation!

Cover-ups! Well, these days we're inclined to think government and local authorities are constantly hiding or burying unflattering reports. During World War Two it was common knowledge and generally accepted by the public that for security reasons the government withheld certain information that might prove, directly or indirectly, detrimental to the nation. In extreme cases of danger we can all understand the need for severe censorship restrictions. But we also are aware that governments can and do cloak material that might embarrass people in high places. I'll give you 'a for instance'...

A former M15 agent named Peter Wright had a book published, dealing with some of his time spent with the organisation. He claimed that the contents did not constitute a belated major threat to the country's security or break open highly confidential files. Regardless of his statement the book was banned and the newspapers were forbidden to publish extracts. The book, printed in Australia and titled "Spycatcher" (great title) was exported all over the world and we at our Dublin retail shops; Camberlys could not keep up with the demand, selling-out book deliveries as soon as they reached the shelves. Naturally, a large number of "Spycatchers" found their way to Britain. I never got to read the book. For me, like my earlier related sardine joke, they were only for buying and selling! I did get to hear from different readers that the contents were much ado about nothing.

I have been asked "apart from Spycatcher what were our best selling books during 'Camberlys' retail operation?
Three numbers stand out and in no particular order, are -

Satanic Verses, by Salman Rushdie
The Road Less Travelled, by M. Scott Peck (first name Morgan).
Iacocca an autobiography, by Lee (Lido Anthony) Iacocca and William Novak.

I never read Satanic Verses. I did try but after twenty or so pages gave up. It was described by some wit as 'The biggest selling, least read book.' The novel, as I gathered from press previews, was a contemporary story of the prophet Muhammed, in line with modern day events. This was considered blasphemous by certain Islamic clerics and individuals and a Fatwa was declared on the author. At our Camberly shops we received telephoned verbal threats from callers we presumed to be Muslims, warning us that to continue stocking the book would result in a reprisal. We made enquiries with certain agencies to ascertain whether the book defamed Muhammed or the Islamic religion, something we would certainly not do and were assured this was not the case.

'The Road Less Travelled' is a book I have read, although in reading the very first chapter one virtually gets the writer's entire message. The opening line begins "Life is difficult ..." and proceeds to say that; until a person accepts and comes to terms with that as a fact; then one is not in a position to deal with the difficulties. The author, M. Scott Peck, considers the route and answer to coping is self-discipline and in accepting responsibility for one's own actions.

Some years ago the psychiatrist who sold over 10,000,000 of the above title was diagnosed with Parkinsons and shortly after this illness came to light his wife of 43 years walked out on him. Perhaps she could not cope with his condition. Facing up to her sudden departure he followed his own advice and accepted she was gone for good. Answering a question about how he felt, his only comment was that her action saddened him. M. Scott Peck died in 2005.

The third excellent seller was Iacocca and a favourite read of mine. Now like me, when I first heard the name in the early/mid 1980s, some of you may say "Io-what"? or even "Io-who"?

Lee Iacocca hit the limelight when he worked as a young executive for the Ford motor company. There he did very well, helping the firm make large profits. In fact he was so successful many people credited him as being the driving force behind the thriving motor manufacturing badge. Most bosses would have been delighted to have such a talented man on board but apparently Mister Ford was not happy to see an underling receive all the plaudits for the company's successes. This inevitably led to a personality clash and in time someone had to go and that was not going to be the boss!

Soon after Iacocca's departure from the Ford Motor Corporation the directors at the Chrysler Corporation, faced with serious problems and facing bankruptcy, called upon Iacocca for help. He was so taken aback at the plight of the company that he made an astounding offer, saying, he would take on the task of sorting out the firms problems for one year on an annual salary of ONE DOLLAR! That's correct, $1.

Here as I write this in 2009, I cannot imagine with all the corporate greed we hear about every day, any notable executive would be willing to make such a similar offer. In addition, Iacocca said he would not take a salary or bonus until the company showed a profit. Nowadays with many car firms in dire financial straits I have not heard of one director who has acted in such a dramatic fashion to help save a company from going down. His book and the telling of how he achieved success, turning a loss making corporation into a profitable one is absorbing, straight talking with no flim-flam. Before moving on here is an interesting note on the man. Years later when it became clear that the Statue of Liberty was in dire need of repair the Mayor and borough authorities asked Iacocca to help raise the necessary millions of dollars to cover the costs. This he willingly did and again did so without seeking money for his time.

For any visitor to Ireland wishing to get an unbiased slant on Irish history, then this book 'A History of Ireland', by Robert Kee, is the one we recommended at Camberlys. Robert Kee, who worked with both the BBC and ITV as interviewer and reporter covers the major happenings from 800 BCE right up to 1994. There are so many misconceptions abroad about the background to Ireland's political upheavals it is refreshing to find a writer who dispassionately gives a fair insight into the major events.

Two other successful selling books for your coffee table are 'Dublin and its People' and 'Ireland and its People'. Both contain excellent photographs, especially the 'Dublin' book with many colourful pictures of the capital around 1980.

On to more modern historic occasions and retuning to the main events of 1986. Prime minister Margaret Thatcher and French President François Mitterand signed an agreement for both countries to build a channel tunnel. A thirty-one mile rail tunnel that took eight years to build. As with the Concorde and Airbus aeroplanes both nations proved they could work together in creating another successful project.

In the same year we went from Anglo/French hand-in-hand cooperation to 'The Hand of God'. Football followers will immediately recognise the controversial remark uttered by the famous Argentinian striker Maradona. In a quarter-final world cup match between England and Argentina in Mexico the brilliant player blatantly handled the ball into the English net. The referee failed to see what happened and awarded a goal, to the fury of the England team and supporters. The Argentinians went on to win the cup.

Still on sport and on a happier note England won the Ashes that year and better still, for me, Liverpool Football Club won the football League Championship and the FA cup, a notable double.

17

MOSCOW MAY DAYS

At the beginning of 1987 Anita and I got to hear first-hand accounts of Russian Jews who were denied permission to leave the Soviet Union. This, despite Soviet Union laws accepting the rights of citizens to come and go without hindrance. Those who were refused exit visas became known as 'Refuseniks' and having read several articles by Bernard Levin in the Times newspaper condemning the way these people were being treated, decided we would go and see for ourselves what was happening.

With the help of 'a friend of a friend of a friend' we got together a list of names, addresses and telephone numbers of Refuseniks living in Moscow. A few advised us also on what small gifts we may wish to bring. So, with a long planned wish to visit the Russian capital we joined a Thompson Travel five day excursion group and set off on a short holiday to Moscow. I kept a note of this trip and for anyone interested in our impressions and the prevailing plight of the Refuseniks in 1987 here are extracts from our 34 paged (A4) account.

Thursday.
A day in May 1987.
Flight BA 710 from London touches down at Moscow Airport. We put our watches forward three hours and stepped back in time thirty years.

Visitors landing in Moscow enter a newish drab building. Inside, the entire place is painted in drab colours and drab green uniforms are filled with drab people. As you may guess the in-colour here is drab. Our first contact with a Soviet is Passport Control. The young uniformed official checks us over carefully. With passport in hand,

slowly, he methodically examines my facial features. He studies in order:
The hairline ... then the passport photograph.
Shape of face ... the passport photograph.
The eyes ... and again, the passport photograph.
My nose ... and yes ... the passport photograph.
The mouth and chin ... the passport photograph.

I smile apologetically, as he does this realising that the Visa photo of Al Capone looks nothing like me! He stares back and tightens his jaw obviously nobody instructed him to smile so smiling is out. It's a good job Anita and I are just two holiday visitors with nothing to fear, or is smiling at an official an offence!

After passport control we head for baggage collection and customs. Our cases arrive quickly and we join one of six or seven queues. Some lines have two or three people checking luggage, yet with only one person handling our line we move much quicker. Past a barrier we meet a smiling face, our courier from Thompson Travel and she is French! Nadine rounds up our party of twenty-eight and heads us towards a coach and the bus begins a forty-five minute trip into Moscow city centre. Along the wide straight roads we drive. Its warmer than we expected and strong sunshine streams through the windows. Everyone sits back and we relax as Nadine explains the hotel arrangements and five day optional programme of tours and events.

The roads and pavements are clean, no litter anywhere. It is like this all over Moscow. Teams of cleaners are constantly engaged to keep the city spotless. To our left a man-made lake and pleasure park. Then a sports stadium further on. One of Moscow's seven main-line railway stations to our right and into Gorki Street, the main street with impressive government buildings. On we go, still enjoying

Nadine's running commentary. Suddenly we arrive at the Rossia Hotel, (pronounced Russia) with six thousand beds it is one of the biggest in the Union. Built in the shape of a squat squared block, each side of the building is a separate hotel in itself. North, East, South, West are divided and we are booked into the Western wing. Our room overlooks the Kremlin wall, Red Square and to the side, the Moscow River.

However, the courier spends 45 minutes checking us into the hotel before we can get to the rooms. In the meantime, we wait in the coach, unable to leave, frying in the sun. Eventually Nadine returns and hands us room cards. These cards entitle us to a room key and their system works like this:
Our guest number is 3050. The first digit indicates the floor, (Ground floor is 1). We take the lift to floor three and at the end of a corridor sits a supervisor behind a desk who takes our card and hands us a key. She then hand writes our arrival time in a large ledger. Should we wish to leave the room we must return to the desk, hand back the key in exchange for the card. Once more the time of our leaving is noted in the big book! We discover in chatting to other guests that everyone is checked in this manner 24 hours a day, on every floor, over four wings. By our estimation this procedure employs at least one hundred and twenty persons for a five day week. Add on staff for weekend and holiday cover and you begin thinking 'Big Brother is alive and well living in the USSR'.

The bedrooms are fair sized but dingy. Everything is coloured in shades of brown. The bed covers and curtains are matching coffee brown. Brown pelmets and brown wooden furniture. Beige wallpaper with brown and beige toned carpets. The mind boggles who designed all of this? It's early hours into our visit and we've more examples of the colourless society to come.

A reminder note: This is my recording of a visit in 1987. Since then Russian hotels may have caught up on Western standards. Still, come with me on a guided tour and a taste of how the Refuseniks were treated.

Our party assemble in the restaurant for a late high-tea cum dinner meal. The meal is plain and by Western standards tasteless. One food item is plentiful, cucumbers. They come with every meal. Like them or not, diners are going to get cucumbers morning noon and night! The presentation of meals is poor and the service worse. Bad service is everyone's gripe. Tipping is discouraged and we learn from locals that good service is seldom seen or expected because high achievement is not recognised nor rewarded. For most workers the common attitude is why bother? Complaints are generally handled by the courier but guests seldom express their grumbles. After coffee we head out for a short walk and make a few phone calls from a list of known Refuseniks. Public telephone kiosks are kept in pristine condition, broken or vandalised booths are unheard of in Moscow. They are also good value, local calls costing two pence. Having made several appointments we head back to the Rossia and retire to bed.

Breakfast next morning consists of rolls, black bread, cheese, followed by an egg based soufflé and black coffee. Already I'm in a bad way for a cup of tea, tea with milk, civilised tea! It's not available in this six thousand bed hotel.

10am. Anita and I board the coach for a city tour. Nadine hands us over to Soviet guide Lena. It appears only Russians are allowed to serve up the propaganda. Lena is good at her job. She knows Moscow well, is intelligent and speaks excellent English with an American accent. First we head up Gorki Street past many state headquarters and one-time homes of famous poets, writers and composers. Many streets are named after revolutionaries. The driver skirts the Kremlin and passes the Olympic stadium. Soon after, we climb steadily and arrive at a scenic vantage point. On our left is the Moscow university, an imposing building. Pupils with the right qualifications receive free tuition. Lena tells us that all education in the USSR is free. Looking to our right and downwards, is a good view of the city.

Back on the coach we learn more facts. Medical treatment is free to all citizens and rents on apartments cost between two and three pounds a week. We discover later, these are small and poorly finished. Wages average about two hundred and fifty pounds a month. General salary scales are narrow and offer little incentive to anyone with real talent, hence as I wrote earlier, the bad service.

Moscow, for those who have not been, is like a less fashionable version of Paris, with avenues, parks and an excellent Metro (subway) system with stations that are spacious, clean and one of the few services well run. The fare for all destinations is about five pence. Buying a travel ticket is simple. One just drops a five Kopek coin into a slot to operate the barrier. No tickets no mess. Each station has a goodly number of cash exchange machines and we wonder why London Underground has not learned from this and the well run Paris system.

There are over seven million inhabitants living in the capital and most use public transport. The most popular car is the Lada and although taxis are plentiful, they are expensive.

After lunch we head to the nearby Metro station with the name Nogina Plascad. The journey takes about thirty minutes and at the station we are met by Karl. Now at no stage am I going to use real names. Yes, I realise I'm writing of a time long past but feel honour bound not to reveal even now, the names of those we met. Karl is in his mid thirties. A gaunt figure, just less than six feet tall, he walks with a slight stoop. At his apartment we are greeted by one of his two sons. Wife Tanya and the remaining son are visiting her sick mother. The apartment is sparsely furnished, untidy but clean. The entire home has bare wooden floors and with little storage space, kiddies shoes are scattered about.

Karl speaks English in a slow measured way. He is pleased to see us and delighted with some books we brought which he looks over with a broad smile. He begins to unwind. Because of his desire to leave Russia he lost his teaching job. This happens a lot to would-be leavers. To make ends meet Karl gives private maths lessons and has been supported mainly by fellow Jews. Recently he has been advised that his application to emigrate is likely to result in a permission to leave. The odds he believes are 80% favourable. He goes on to tell us, in general there is much difficulty and confusion with regard to gaining exit permits. The rules keep changing and more recent requests to leave have met with stiffer conditions with the authorities requesting evidence of applicants having 'direct relatives abroad'. The Visa office meaning of 'a direct relative' is father, mother, brother, sister, son or daughter.

Two hours later we move on to meet a lovely couple. They live in a slightly better apartment. In the living room the floor is partly covered with a thin square carpet and there is a small twin couch and two easy chairs. Two of the walls are lined ceiling to floor with books, mostly in English, over a wide range of subjects. Among the titles are recent publications which I learned afterwards have been sent by sympathisers in Britain. Josef and Tina are a cosy looking middle-aged couple. The husband, who is of medium height, slim, and smart speaks good precise English. Tina is fair and plump with a ready smile. Her husband (a scientist) talks evenly without passion. We speak about 'Glasnost', a term translated from the Russian language, meaning 'openness and transparency in the activities of all Soviet government institutions with freedom of information'.

Josef smiles. “At this stage its too early to see what game Gorbachev is playing. He has problems of a great size and needs co-operation from the West as he tries to open up the Soviet economy, within limits. The pace at which he can move is also limited. With us, a small cog in the whole scheme of things, it is difficult to see where we come into the reckoning. An important element also is how will the Western powers react to our plight? Will they seize the opportunity to say “How can we trust a country that talks of 'Glasnost' but denies its citizens basic human rights”?

Josef goes on to say he welcomes the increase in emigration figures but is concerned about the 'long term refuseniks' who have been shunted to one side. I ask him to enlarge upon that statement. He explains that broadly, Jews of any high position in computers, medicine, science and engineering are most likely to be frustrated in their attempts to leave the country. As a scientist he falls into that category. His son Yuri, a student, has been allowed to leave and is living in Israel. So, although he and Tina can claim to have a 'direct relative abroad', his previous employment in a science lab has affected their application. I say 'previous employment' because the moment anyone applies for a visa they lose their job, regardless of what the work entailed.

We take a note of son Yuri's address in Israel and determine, with his help, to draw media attention to their situation upon our return to Dublin. Before leaving Josef phones a friend and makes an appointment for us to visit another flat within walking distance.

Mikhail and Elena greet us warmly. They are in their late twenties to early thirties and have two lovely sons aged four and six. Elena is expecting number three in early September. An Orthodox family, they speak Hebrew at home. Mikhail is tall, sandy complexion and friendly in a shy way. His English is not good but he tries hard to express his thoughts. He has been learning English from yellowed pages torn from some ancient text book. Elena is an attractive young woman and she is able to communicate with Anita in French. The couple are keen to live in Israel and the Russian officials seemingly are not happy with that. He too has lost his job and finds the only work available for him are menial tasks like street cleaning, or portering. He and the other Refuseniks with fine intelligent minds are humbled in this way. I don't mean to infer they have lost respect for themselves. In every case we came across there were examples of improvisation and determination to beat the odds stacked against them. As with other Refuseniks who lost their jobs he now gives private lessons. His childrens' classes are for religious instruction and are well attended.

Listening to the various stories, all with a common theme, we are puzzled by the Soviet attitude, denying people the freedom to emigrate. So widespread is the problem that the British TV station Channel 4 have produced a moving documentary on the problems would-be emigrants face, titled 'No Exit'. This excellent film produced by Ken Howard is narrated by Bernard Levin.

Saturday

In the morning, Anita and I joined a Thompson Travel tour of the Kremlin, a name meaning 'Fortress'. The Kremlin dates back to the 15th century and is surrounded by a wall approximately eight metres high, in the heart of the city. The red bricked wall is two and a half kilometres long and within this boundary is the Presidium where the government sits securely, close to a well patrolled barracks quarter for armed guards. The Kremlin has three entrances, one solely for government officials. The actual parliament building is sealed off from tourists with the remaining places of interest, consisting of five old, well kept churches highlighted by the guide for photographing. None of these buildings are used for prayers. The multi-turnip domed buildings are little more than pretty museums, situated around a square but not open to citizens or visitors. Outwardly, as museums they are nice reminders of days gone by, not that the Czars and Czarinas were much to admire or fondly remember.

The only church we are allowed into lies outside the Kremlin entrance. It is Saint Basil's and it faces the length of Red Square. Inside we see many pieces of silver fashioned in crosses, goblets, and alter decorations. The interior, like the outside is kept in good repair except for the religious wall paintings. These have been allowed to fade and we are told by the guide it's because few Russians are interested in religion. We find out, this is not true and that Christians are are trying hard to open or reopen churches. Despite rigid controls on religious services the number of baptisms and church weddings are on the increase. Some church leaders, a few, are gaining more freedom to worship.

Out in Red Square and half way along the Kremlin wall is the Lenin Mausoleum. We watch the strange (to us) custom of several newly-wed couples among a long queue, waiting, we are informed, to pay their respects. This we also gather will bring good luck to their future. In Mother Russia a civil wedding ceremony is simple. A politician or well known member of the communist party or even a senior respected person, is invited to address the couple. This address, wishing them good health, a happy future and children, may be held anywhere, usually in front of family and close friends in a dwelling or during the summer months in a park. The bride usually wears a simple white outfit, the man a suit. Traditionally, the Best Man and Best Woman wear wide red satin waist bands. When the dignitary has imparted his short message the couple exchange rings.

They are now husband and wife. Champagne is poured to toast the couple, who share a glass. Later Mr. and Mrs Anonovich do a walkabout, stroll through the park, visit their favourite spot or as we've watched, called upon Lenin!

After our park visit we ask the tour guide if most dating couples end up getting married or are now following western trends of just living together, with no civil or religious bindings. The general trend is for couples to marry at a younger age than in Britain and Ireland but divorce rates are high, at least 50% marriages fail within a couple of years.

Crowds of uniformed children appear. Boys and girls, smartly dressed in white shirts, red ties and black trousers or skirts. They are the Russian equivalent of scouts, called Pioneers. They have been bussed into Red Square where they listen to tales of the revolutionary struggles. Joining youth movements, joining in marriage, all paths lead to Lenin!

Anita and I have no interest in seeing inside Lenin's Mausoleum. We just watch the changing of the goose-stepping guard which takes place on the hour.

Across Red Square sits Moscow's biggest store 'Gum'. Before describing that place I should mention a wee fact; the Square is not a square, it is oblong shaped and the Russian meaning of 'Red' is beautiful. So perhaps Red Square should be renamed 'Beautiful Oblong'!

The Gum store claimed by Muscovites to be the largest in the world is more like a big market place. The most massive, super dooper market place in the universe, if one wishes to title it but by Western standards a store it ain't. Inside this large building are kiosks, open stalls, small shops with a handful of larger retail outlets. Near the main entrance there is a long queue. It trails around a corner for twenty metres and the would-be buyers are waiting to purchase purses. Good quality clothes are hard to find and anything nice in knitwear is expensive. A dull coloured sleeveless pullover (probably "shoddy" - reclaimed wool) sells for fifty pounds, (1987 price).

Food prices are low but supplies are hard to come by. Queues for fruit and vegetables are common and we are told meat has been absent in most parts for the past three days. Items such as camera film, batteries, tea and coffee are also hard to get and women complain about the hours spent standing in long lines. This is the scene in 1987, similar to the wartime and immediate post war period in Britain.

The evening hotel meal is no better than our first day's experience and our taste buds have gone into hibernation. We nibble at rolls and cucumber. Except for the odd grumble rumble, my tummy is not speaking to me. After the meal we go for a walk with an English couple. They have been advised that all the hotel rooms are bugged. An exaggeration? Perhaps, but we're inclined to believe 'Big Brotherofsky' is more than alive and well in Russia. This inclination is reinforced next day when we set out to visit more Refuseniks.

Our hotel is about a kilometre from the Metro station and on the way Anita stops to look in a corner shop window. I see little of interest and as we walk on she tells me we're being followed. "At the last street crossing I noticed a man walking behind us. When we stopped just now he also stopped and bent to fiddle with his white trainers. I'm sure he's out to see where we're going today.

With that, at the next turning I drew a map from my pocket and stopped to look around as if checking street names and so on. The man now moved to the kerb and stood waiting for traffic to pass as if intending to cross to the far side. I checked on his appearance and we carried on.

Inside the metro station entrance we walked down a short flight of steps and through glass push doors. We stopped suddenly, ahead of the escalators and stood by the wall waiting. Almost at once the man came into view again, down the stairs he too halted but on the other side of the glass doors. This was now looking serious and we decided not to proceed any further but to wait and see how long he would stand in our view. I checked my watch. He stood idle for fully eight minutes, then moving quickly came through the doors and disappeared down the escalator. We waited another ten minutes before moving on. At the platform there were few people about and positively no sign of our follower.

Our journey took just over twenty minutes and all the prepared calls lay close to each other. At the first calling we met among a group of eight people, one was one of the most well known Refuseniks in the Soviet Union. This person had heard of our visit and travelled on a devious route from a small town on the outskirts of Moscow to meet us. It proved for us to be a very humbling experience. A long term campaigner for other peoples' rights, our new acquaintance told of how they had been beaten, jailed and isolated in their home town. Freed after months of detention, the telephone service had been disconnected and even now the post was being censored. Anita and I were asked if we would contact the town mayor, demanding to know why this person's phone line had been cut dead. This we did on our return and were pleased to learn the service was restored soon after.

During our visit everyone in the room joined in a free flowing exchange of stories and although many were of a similar nature; the Visa Office kept moving the goalposts thereby creating fresh reasons for blocking exit permits. In the majority of cases the refusals were given verbally.

At the end of a meeting that went on till midnight we were asked if we could return the next day to meet with others in the same 'tied' situation. The reason for asking us to come back was quite simple. The Refuseniks depended a lot on outsiders to draw attention in the West to their dilemma. The more voices raised on their behalf helped increase the number of exit permits.

In a world where citizens of one country are generally prevented from entering other lands it seemed odd that the Soviets should stop anyone wishing to leave for a place where they'll be welcomed.

Back at the hotel and shortly after 1am the telephone rang. When I answered there was a brief silence, then a thick foreign accent said, “Mr. Samwell”? I replied “yes” and asked who was calling. There was another pause and the line went dead. I motioned to Anita not to talk and whispered to her what was said. Or more precisely, what was not said. A strange call at 1am. We wondered about it and the man who seemed to follow us that morning. Over-hyped imagination? Coincidence? Or someone trying to frustrate us? Whatever the story we decided to use our final full day in Moscow seeing more Refuseniks as promised.

Monday - A day we would never forget. It was a worrying day. A day of sadness and one to remember of brave, warm people who would never cease fighting for justice and the right to leave Russia.

Here once more, in writing of those who came to see us, I'll refrain from mentioning real names or for that matter, pseudonyms.

Straight after breakfast on a beautiful sunny morning we made for the metro. By now we were accustomed to the system and didn't need to study the signs, most of which were in Russian. Moving speedily to the escalator we both noticed two men at the bottom, one with a shoulder movie camera pointing in our direction.

Anita became quite agitated. Pointing, she said, “They're aiming that thing at us”. It certainly looked that way and I wondered what would happen when we reached where they stood. Close to the bottom with the camera angle now clearly dropping in line with our descent the men suddenly turned and ran down the platform. To my utter astonishment Anita went chasing after them! She returned a few minutes later.

“Did you see that? The stocky one was filming us”!
I took her arm. “What on earth were you thinking of ... chasing him”?
“I wanted to see where he was going but he just ran up some stairs and vanished”. To my way of thinking the man had made it too obvious what he was doing and I reassured Anita that his performance was just that, an obvious dramatic performance to scare us. “If the police or security people really wanted to secretly film us, believe me, we would not have got the slightest hint or sight of them”. I continued to ease her concerns. “This little staged act was intended for us to see them. A deterrent perhaps? We'll never know”.

Feeling a little uneasy, we agreed to carry on with what was to be our final call. At the apartment another group of eight people were assembled and in turn told us of their individual attempts to leave Moscow. One couple had just been informed 'the recent application was refused and not be re-considered until 1993'. Six years from now! Their early hopes and expectations that the newly declared Glasnost might ease the usual delaying process now lay in tatters and it showed on their faces. Quietly they asked if we could bring their story to the attention of friends in England and perhaps approach some Irish politicians to support them. We readily agreed. How we went about our promise is covered in a later chapter.

An Orthodox husband and wife whose lives were turned upside down related how badly they and a daughter were treated as a result of a composition written by the girl aged 15. This took place four or five years ago and here is the man's account of what followed.

Our daughter's class were asked to write a piece on the word 'Mother'. She wrote a lengthy article saying how fortunate she was, because she had three mothers, going on to extol in depth how good this made her feel.

Firstly the Mother who bore and brought her into the world.
Secondly Mother Russia, the land of her birth.
Thirdly Israel, her spiritual Mother.

The teacher sent for the school head and the girl's work was read out. Then the head denounced her as a traitor to the Soviet Union. The youngster was subjected to massive humiliation by the teachers and afterwards, when she suffered beatings at the hands of fellow students the school board took no action to protect her. On the contrary they acquired what is called in Russia, "Soviet blindness", translated for you as ignoring agreed and stated rules.

That was not the end of the matter, far from it. When the father was refused yet again an exit visa, he found it impossible to get even menial work. In desperation he demonstrated outside government offices and was arrested for slander against the state. Because he could not trust a state provided lawyer he elected at court to defend himself. Before the trial he spent days swotting up on laws that he felt applied to his case.

The case proceeded slowly, the prosecutor dwelling on his desire to leave the Soviet Union and the arrogant manner in which he attacked the USSR. His reply was straightforward. He only applied for something that was within his legal rights and this did not violate the state or other citizens.

The prosecution then called his daughter forward as a material witness, against the father. When she refused to testify, her composition was read out in court with the prosecutor claiming her mind had been poisoned by the father. It was a ridiculous accusation but the judge thought otherwise and brought in a guilty verdict, sentencing the man to 3 years in jail! A full three years with no remission, for a private, peaceful demonstration.

The laws of the Soviet Union allow prisoners a minimum of two family visits a year. This Man was allowed one! In jail he suffered heart problems and is now dependent on daily heart tablets.

Throughout this meeting we heard similar stories, some told in quiet even tones, some in excitable outbursts. Calm voices, explosive voices. Young and not so young people all unloading pent-up frustrations. To apply for a visa leads to immediate job dismissal. No job ... no pay. Without a job a person might be charged with being a 'parasite' and parasites may be sent to a labour camp, the regimes answer to unemployment. As for 'glasnost' the Refuseniks termed this - "Gorbachev's propaganda for Western consumption".

There are shortages of many things in the Soviet Union but no shortage of state rules and these change, as the officials wish them to change. After listening to the views of those we met, like them, we could not make sense out of what Glasnost really stands for. Winston Churchill said back in 1939, "I cannot forecast to you the action of Russia. It is a riddle wrapped in a mystery inside an enigma".

That evening we left behind us fine, brave people with promises to bring as much attention to their individual cases as we could, our heads spinning with names and facts to remember. We knew our first task would begin the moment we got aboard the plane for home, making copious notes.

Tuesday morning; the same set breakfast. We'll always associate cucumbers with Moscow. The coach gets us back to the airport quickly and strangely the terminal seems smaller than we first thought. We have to check-out through the customs. Some passengers are searched thoroughly, one young woman for fifteen minutes. To get a drink or sandwich is difficult. One tiny bar operated by two slow moving attendants making no effort to cope with a small queue of impatient travellers. We sit and compare observations with other passengers. At last we board our BA plane, greeted by a lovely stewardess and allowed a choice of UK newspapers. We catch up with the news. 'Coventry beat Tottenham Hotspur in the FA cup-final'. A surprise. 'Maggie Thatcher and Neil Kinnock prepare for the coming election'. No surprise.

Sometime later a voice over the intercom announces, “Ladies and Gentlemen we have just left Soviet air space”. Everyone cheers. I close my eyes ... not to sleep but to think. We're glad to be going home. What can we do back in Dublin to help those we met? I can still see their faces and remember their names. I open my eyes and begin writing and Anita does the same.

18

PUBLICITY

The boisterous Irish writer Brendan Behan said of the word publicity, "All publicity is good, except an obituary notice".

When I was on a business consultancy course in Stroud (photo below) a man steeped in advertising claimed there was no such thing as bad publicity. In his opinion any kind of publicity surrounding anything or anyone who caught the eye and made people think or talk was successful because of the attention drawn.

Urwick Orr Business Consultancy Course in Stroud, 1965

On the heels of our Moscow visit Anita and I sat down to discuss how we would follow up with our promises to focus more attention on the plight of the Refuseniks. Our first act lead us on an interesting and successful course when I made contact with the London friend of a Refusenik. The man told me of his recent overtures to sympathetic British members of parliament and of letters published in the national press. He also informed me that Alex, the adult son of a couple whom we had met, was staying for a brief time at his home working to draw attention to his parents' case. They were the husband and wife who had been notified that their application to leave Russia would not be reconsidered for another six years. Alex, now an Israeli citizen, was prepared to do anything to help his parents. I immediately offered to send him an air ticket to Dublin and for him to stay with us and assist in maximising our efforts in Ireland.

When Alex arrived in Dublin we were pleased to find he spoke excellent English. Our son Colin proposed we get in touch with the radio producers of a current affairs programme presented by Pat Kenny. This was a popular morning broadcast with a large listening audience. No time was lost in contacting the programme makers and to our relief, with short notice, they agreed for Alex to visit the studio, tell his story and be interviewed by Kenny. To his great credit Pat Kenny not only gave full prominence to the problems faced by Alex's parents but also explored the dire straits of all the would-be emigrants. The whole episode went so well that Alex and ourselves were delighted.

Our next big break came when the Irish member of parliament Ben Briscoe took a strong interest in our quest. Ben, son of a well known former Irish parliamentarian, Robert Briscoe (and both elected Lord Mayors of Dublin) was instrumental in Alex getting to meet other politicians at Dáil Éireann, the Irish parliament house.

Both he and a colleague also attended our home reception organised especially for Alex to meet members of the Dublin Jewish community. The enjoyable evening was really intended as a morale boosting exercise, letting the young man know there were other people behind the scenes supporting his and our efforts to gain an early exit visa for his parents.

The next day, again with our political friends, we had a meeting with the Irish Minister for Foreign Affairs. This we felt was very productive, especially when told that a direct appeal would be made to the minister's Soviet counterpart.

During the same period we were aware that other people in Britain and Ireland were working along similar lines drawing constant attention to other cases and there is little doubt the wide clamour, like that of another ethnic demand and cry of “Let my people go” had an effect on the weary Soviet emigration office officials.

To our satisfaction, within a year we had a lovely letter from Alex's parents to say that despite the earlier warning that their exit application would not be reviewed for six years they were now happily living in Israel with job prospects for both of them lined up.

More confirmations of successful emigrations followed and I'm sure the exodus did little to harm the Russian economy. So, why did they not relent sooner? In a society which claimed all citizens had a right to free passage why pick on and deny that right to the Jews? Sounds like an old familiar question.

19

BLACK MONDAY - BLACK TIMES

Adults living in Britain during 1987 are likely to remember the catalogue of disasters that hit the nation like a series of plagues. It began one evening in March when on a calm sea a car-ferry named 'Herald of Free Enterprise' capsized in fairly shallow water less than a kilometre from the harbour at Zeebrugge. The cross channel ship with almost seven hundred people on board was heading for Dover with its bow doors not fully shut. As it picked up speed water poured onto the car decks and with each slight roll of the ship the canting side to side movement of water gained rapid momentum. It took just minutes for the gathering weight to turn the boat on its side. Because the terrible disaster happened so close to shore Belgian rescue teams were quickly on the scene. They and those passengers who managed to get free made heroic efforts to rescue many trapped passengers. By next early morning it was announced that 193 people had lost their lives.

Tragic events, such as the sinking of a ship are always followed by an enquiry in order to establish what causes lead to the accident. In time, a lengthy inquest determined that hurried actions to turn the ship around for its return journey caused some crew to ignore or forget safety practices. The bow doors were not closed properly and no one seemed to double-check or notice such an important function was not carried out. The reasons for more dreadful deaths during the year revolved around the ongoing conflicts in Northern Ireland. Two major occurrences resulted in violent killings. Eight I.R.A. men were shot dead during a raid on a police station and in November, at a Remembrance Day parade in the town of Enniskillen and on what is now referred to as The Poppy Day Massacre, the I.R.A. detonated a bomb killing 11 and injuring 60, including women and children.

Another massacre, with no political agenda attached, happened at the peaceful town of Hungerford in Berkshire. There, a so-called gun enthusiast went on a rampage killing 16 men, women and children. The press described it as Britain's worst ever mass shooting incident.

I cannot recollect if anyone ever discovered the motive as to why a young man went out, shot indiscriminately at whoever crossed his path, set his home alight and when cornered by the police shot himself.

The 'black' stories of 1987 that I've just written about are remembered by most adults who lived during those times. One calamity concerning the often discussed topic 'the weather' is also well remembered, except for the extent of the total horror it created. I'm referring to The Great Gale.

Around the middle of October the BBC weather presenter Michael Fish said in an early evening report that a woman had phoned the station to say she had heard the country was in the path of a tremendous hurricane. Fish smiled and said there was no chance of the storm affecting Britain. The official announcement and the fact that it was so wide of the mark is, like I said, something many people remember. However, present-day impressions on the number of deaths and amount of devastation the hurricane left in its wake seem to have dimmed. At least 17 people were killed and hundreds injured when winds of over 177km/h (110 mph) hit the south of England. I remember that figure 17 loomed large in the statistics surrounding the deaths and destruction; 17 killed; 177km/h winds; 17 million trees destroyed.

A few days later, a new media headline was coined. It was 'Black Monday'. On Monday 19th October, the bottom fell out of the London stock exchange when £50 billion was wiped off the value of shares in a matter of hours. Later that same day in New York the Dow Jones suffered even bigger losses, bringing an end to a five year run of bullish growth. You know, when you've lived long enough this kind of happening gets to seem quite familiar. In the words of Paul Harvey, an American radio commentator, “In times like these it helps to recall there have always been times like these”!

The press and economic gurus, or whatever the current name is credited to so-called experts announce how the 'crisis' came about. With deep convoluted analysis of the factors behind the collapse the views expressed are more often than not uttered by the very same people who 24 hours earlier, like the BBC weather expert Michael Fish, never had an inkling of the whirlwind about to strike.

Words like overvalued stocks, recession, imbalances within computer networks, imbalances in national budgets, resulting in loss of confidence and other high blown reasons were and still are bandied about. Then, when time passes and things pick up again the financial experts and the politicians announce; “There will be no more boom and bust”.

Excuse me while I break off here with a fit of ironic laughter. Gordon Brown has been recorded in 'Hansard' (the official reporting of all proceedings in the House of Commons) as saying; “There will be no more boom and bust” over 100 times in the the House of Commons. Of course when the bad days returned and as a result of government over-spending, there were no reserves to fall back on, the blame for the 'bust' was laid elsewhere.

Back in 1955 an old and wise salesman named James Cummings (not an economic genius) calmed a young Roy who was concerned about the present day recession. He asked me if I knew the old testament story of Joseph, the multi-coloured coat hero and of how he interpreted the king's dreams, saying the kingdom would face the coming years with “7 years fat and 7 years lean”.

“Well Roy, life doesn't quite follow those precise lengths but just like a pendulum we shall always experience economic swings, one way, then the other and all the wizards of Wall Street, the City of London, Frankfurt and Zurich won't change it”.

The way I've clumped together this chapters' reminiscences and stories may suggest that I saw 1987 as an exceptionally black year. Looking back, my impressions are likely to have been affected by what followed in the Autumn of that year.

The first signs that all was not well with my Brother Melvyn's health happened in October. This came out of the blue since he was always very active and despite a one time arthritic problem that burned out, he was playing tennis on a regular basis. After several medical checks he mentioned that there were signs of fluid in the lungs that might need to be drained. Because he did not smoke the diagnosis puzzled me somewhat but at the time he did not seem overly concerned and said that should anyone inquire or talk of circulating rumours regarding his health, the 'lung fluid' story was to be the stock answer.

I cannot say for certain when the hospital treatments began but in between these times he was still playing tennis through the Winter. It was also during that period that our Dad suffered what the medics described as “a mild to medium stroke”. During one week I remember visiting Melvyn at Saint Vincent's hospital and then going straight on to see Da at Mercers Hospital. Of the two patients, our Dad seemed to be in the poorer condition, especially as his memory banks were almost blank. For days my Mother and I spent ages feeding him family names and facts reminding him of who was who, places where he and everyone else lived and worked. We brought in newspapers and taught his child-like mind to read again. Although I had seen Anita's father suffer years back in a similar way every stroke affects one differently. Slowly, ever so slowly, Da regained his mental faculties and health.

Into 1988 and my Brother's health worsened. His daughters Fiona and Michele returned from England to lend support to their Mum, Avril. They along with my Parents and the rest of the family were beginning to realise that cancer lay at the root of Melvyn's ill health. However, for a time it was unclear just how far the ailment had spread. When the chemotherapy treatments began we all realised the situation looked far more serious than first indications showed. Then, in April, Melvyn was seriously impaired with a severe stroke that left him completely paralysed down his left side. For the next four months he battled with a range of handicaps to an extent that baffled the staff at the Elm Park Hospital. Eventually the illness overtook his tremendous brave fight and in the early hours of the 29th August, with Avril, Fiona, Michele, Colin and me at his side he passed peacefully away.

'August is a wicked month'.
The title of a novel by the popular Irish writer Edna O'Brien.
I've never understood how the adjective 'wicked' can be applied to a month. But having said that, in no other period of my life have I hurt so badly as I did in August 1988. For every member of the Family my dear Brother's passing was a crippling blow. For me personally it was like part of my physical being had been removed. I have often said 'twins could not have been closer' and even that description does not satisfy me.

Months later Anita and I were at a trade show in Birmingham where I met an ex-scouting friend named David Stein. He had left Dublin years earlier and not having known Anita I introduced him to her. His opening words to her were, "When I think back to my scouting days, I always remember Roy as being one of the most capable and reliable of people. Someone I could depend on for help or advice".

His flattering description highlighted the difference in my attitude between then and 1988. It may be that my indifferent mood to most things had something to do with efforts to help my Parents cope with their tragic upset at losing a son. Whatever the psychological reasons were, I had sunk to a situation where nothing much seemed to matter any more. When a staff member came to see me regarding their concern over some issue, my off-handed response went something like, "Do you really believe that's a problem"? It was no proper way for me to respond, but, that was how I treated most issues, with no interest in day to day plans, actions, successes or difficulties.

The year of 1988 was drawing to an end. Few daily news happenings during the 12 months caught my attention, except for a couple of dreadful occurrences. The first was when 167 men lost their lives in a huge explosion at the Piper Alpha oil rig off the East coast of Scotland. The catastrophe, considered one of the worst offshore explosions, completely destroyed the rig and an inquest determined the deaths and destruction were caused by leaking gas being ignited.

The second incident is more remembered in detail because of the evil premeditated planning that went towards killing 270 people. Today we know it as the 'Lockerbie Bombing'.

The small Scottish border town of Lockerbie, virtually unknown until this time, lies under the flight path of many cross-Atlantic journeys and in late December a Pan-Am airline 747 Boeing Jumbo Jet, en-route from London to New York exploded high in the sky. The fully fuelled aircraft fell like a fireball from the sky killing all 259 crew and passengers. Another 11 townspeople died when their homes were hit by falling debris. About twenty homes were damaged and the wreckage covered a widespread 800 square miles. A most haunting photograph that frequently crops up is of the front cockpit portion of the fuselage in a deep crater. It is the largest recovered remnant of the Jumbo and what always strikes me is that some of the windows are intact. The front port-side shows three unbroken windows and how they remained intact amazes me.

A team of investigators pored over whatever they could examine and were able to tell that the explosion was caused by a bomb hidden inside a cassette player that had in turn been packed in a suitcase. After years of evidence gathering, the American investigators named two Libyan nationals as suspects behind the crime. Many people believed whoever was responsible had the backing of the Libyan leader Colonel Gaddafi, who refused to extradite the men for trial. After prolonged political discussions the two suspects were brought to trial in Holland with a Scottish judge presiding. One man was jailed for life in 2001 and the alleged accomplice set free.

The single bright patch about that time was when Colin called by one evening as we were dining and introduced us to a bright and pretty young lady whom we'd never seen before. Her name; Gayle Noyek. "You may know of my parents" she said; "Aubrey and Vivienne". I smiled broadly. "Your father Aubrey and I slept in prams, side by side as our parents socialised and from time to time, took turns 'baby sitting' and as very young kids we played at being soldiers".

I reckoned Gayle's father was most likely my first pal and now decades later here was his daughter, keeping company with Colin. How many times have I typed the words " Life is full of coincidences"?

That evening's cheering lift to my spirits did little to improve my outlook in business matters. The commercial motor that normally drove me with great enthusiasm had slipped into neutral. This state of mind continued into the Spring of 1989 until Colin, Peter, Ian and Neal, along with Anita held a meeting behind my back to discuss the current state of Family and business affairs.

20

PASSOVER MOVEOVER

In a previous book I told of an important happening that took place long ago, on the eve of the Jewish festival of Passover. A night when the service and traditional meal is always preceded with the set question, “Why is this night different from all other nights”?

The answer to the perennial call leads to a retelling of how the Jews escaped from slavery in Egypt and returned to their promised land of Israel. But back then our normal evening procedure took on an additional twist of fate that changed our lives. In Book 1 “Sailing Through Plate Glass Doors” that episode was covered fully in a chapter headed “The Man Who Came To Dinner”.

Well, another major turn of events occurred on the eve of Passover 1989. Before the commencement of the evening's proceedings Colin approached me and quietly said that later, when we had finished, Peter would take my Parents home and without their knowing return for a meeting with Anita, me, and our four Sons. So, that night around 11.30pm the six of us sat at the dining table once more as Colin took the chair for our special Family discussion.

Briefly, Colin summed up both Cambie Wholesale and the Camberlys businesses. Despite a good increase in Cambie sales, the net profit result was disappointing. This according to our accountants, was because of the high tax-take. A similar situation applied with our retail division Camberlys. Over the year all six of us worked very hard and he felt the rewards were not good enough. This point led him to say that even with more substantial increases in sales he could not see personal ambitions being realised. With a national population of just under four million the wholesale business would pretty soon reach its maximum sales potential. And unless the retail expanded to at least twice its present size the same sales restrictions would kick-in. Then Colin brought out his big card. Looking to me he said, “Since Melvyn passed on, you have lost interest in the retail business. That is not meant as a critical judgement but it is a fact. We can all see it in your daily work and that too has to be faced when we look to the future. In a nutshell, if we are all to go forward as a Family in business, then it won't happen in Dublin”.

Colin's forthright assessment had clearly been discussed earlier with his Brothers and that view was reinforced when he laid down an alternative proposal to our present situation. He continued, “In order to increase sales substantially we need a bigger market base. That means a move to England and the two best sites for our kind of operation are probably London and Manchester. To properly gauge the best site would require two of us, probably you and me, to visit both and make comparisons taking into account -
Available business and private property sites and costs.
Good road and service networks, with handy access to a major airport.
Closeness to leisure facilities and places of interest”.

In the course of less than five minutes, I felt almost physically uprooted. For sure, my mind was travelling fast, taking in Colin's presentation and trying quickly to weigh up my own immediate reactions. I could see by Anita's expression she had no reservations about the proposals. The first question that leapt to my mind was “What sort of a timetable do you have in mind”?
His reply was quick and precise.
“Within the next two weeks, you and I will visit London and Manchester, not together but separately, so that we can compare independently made notes. Once we've agreed on a place we'll plan to make our first move, by June.

By now, I had more questions in line and began saying -
“I take it you're talking about ... this June”!
He nodded, and I continued.
“Right, obviously you have formed an entire scenario of how we as a Family, with two distinct businesses and three homes, move from Dublin to somewhere in England, in the space of THREE months. How do you see that happening within such a short span of time”?
Briefly, Colin's outlined plan went as follows:
Inside two weeks, he and I having completed our investigative trips to London and Manchester, would decide where to settle in the UK. The Family would then be split into two teams with Colin, Anita, and Ian responsible for renting temporary living accommodation, finding a suitable business address and opening new customer and supplier accounts, within three months - quite a challenge.

Equally daunting, was the longer programme set for our other team of Peter, Neal and me.
Over a period of 15 months we were to -
Advertise and sell three private properties.
Advertise and sell the retail shops as a group or individually.

As surprised as I was by the presentation, I found the prospect of a fresh start in life exciting. Yes, it was going to be a huge moving exercise with a lot of pressure on each individual, but there was little doubt in my mind, the Family was equal to the task and I said so. This affirmation pleased everyone. There was though, just one matter of concern and that was to do with my Parents. Although they were born and raised in Liverpool, lived there until their marriage in 1933, they were now getting on in years and well settled in Dublin. Still, looking at the overall situation, I thought it might be best for them to join us in the move. Naturally, it was going to be for them to decide on whether to uproot and join the six of us. For them, Anita and me, there were going to be a lot of emotional tugs of the heart. We thought about our very close friends and of how we would miss each other; the gaps our move might create bothered us. On one of our move-planning chats Anita admitted that the thought of saying good-bye was one she could not face. One practical solution we felt was to have an apartment in Dublin. A place we and our sons could use on frequent return visits. Through no fault of ours, the well intended idea did not happen, as you will read later.

Working to plan, Colin and I paid separate visits to London and Manchester and concluded without any doubts, that the latter was going to be our new hometown and place of work. The choice came quite easily. Manchester was growing rapidly with an excellent network of motorways, a large international airport, and a city similar in size to Dublin, It lay close to the Lake District, the Peak District, the beauty areas of North Wales, seaside resorts and other pleasant places of interest. There was also a big Jewish community with schools that rated high on the national league table. On top of that, a most important factor was that house and commercial property prices were much lower than London. The final decision was taken quickly and by June Colin, Ian and Anita were on their way.

Anita was no sooner on site when she landed a very large opening order from Waterstones store in St. Ann's Square. The order came so quickly and before Colin had organised the renting of a business premises that we had to make the delivery from Dublin. A promising beginning, before the beginning!!

In the previous two decades and in years to come many friends also emigrated from the Emerald Isle. They left for a variety of reasons and to a variety of different places. Childhood friends Abe Baker, Willy Malkinson, Michael Josephson, Arnold 'Butch' Isaacson, Philip Rifkin, Adele and Philip Turk, Vivienne Jay-Levey, were later followed by Joyce and Joseph Levy, Shirley and Ralph Morris,

Benita and Zally Barnett, Dave and Hilda Solomons, Rose and Aubrey Yodaiken and our dear Elaine Bloom. Their new addresses spread over a wide area. From London and Manchester, to Australia, Canada, Israel and the United States. Why? Well as I've just written, for a variety of reasons.

Pressed as I was by a fellow trader at the Westbury Mall, who was aware communal numbers were declining, he sought an explanation. I struggled to give just one reason. A number of factors lay behind the steady exodus that saw Dublin's Jewish congregation shrink from a post-war total of 4,500 souls to approximately 750 by 2009.

Inside the wider national population, with a democratic system of politics, steady economic conditions and acceptable levels of moderate religious tolerance, a thriving ethnic community such as the Dublin Jewish body once was, depends inwardly on a structure of religious, educational, charitable, sporting and social support groups to bind its own different cultural and moneyed layers of society. With all those factors favourably in place you can understand why it was difficult to come up with a simple answer, especially since everyone who ever lived there claimed how wonderful a place it was ... and I personally would agree. Perhaps my own family goals and aspirations might apply to some leavers, while for others a desire to see their children grow within a larger Jewish mix of people in order to avoid or lessen the risk of assimilation, could be sufficient grounds to move away.

When in the 1950s a moderate reduction of communal members took place with several families going to the newly established state of Israel or England (because of the recession in Ireland) the eroding ripple effect began in earnest, with a slow but steady decline in numbers. Eventually, it became harder for the community to maintain the excellent care-home for the elderly and sporting facilities previously enjoyed. Youth groups dwindled to extinction and major social functions like charitable dinner-dances, quiz nights and concerts became just events to fondly remember.

21

CLOSING DOWN

As I begin this chapter the calender reads April 2009. Britain and Ireland, Europe and America, in fact the whole world, is suffering a tremendous financial downturn.

The large nationwide chain of Woolworths stores, established in Britain for ninety-nine years closed recently along with other well known retail names. If you're wondering why I'm telling you something you're already aware of, well this is the reason.

The greater number of those reading this story will (fortunately) never have experienced what it is like to either lose one's job or, be responsible for closing a business and the jobs that go with it. The Woolworths closures were reported in the press and on television in great detail. Subsequent stories touched on the impact these close-downs had on staff and management alike, an experience I faced in 1989.

My carefully laid out plans to withdraw from the retail trade could not have been better prepared or more simple. So I believed. Oh yes, the best laid plans can certainly go to pot!

The first stage in the programme was to tell senior staff members of my intention to sell all the Camberly units as going concerns, preferably to one buyer and to retire from the retail trade. This I would do with imminent suitable advertisements in the 'Irish Independent' newspaper. To coincide with that our biggest suppliers would be asked to call so I could explain our intentions and reassure them the existing firm would continue trading in its present form until a new handover took place.

On the very next morning, following my telephoned notice to our main supplier, I had an immediate appointment for 11am at the Westbury Hotel coffee shop. The sales manager smilingly introduced me to a younger man saying "It's a coincidence Roy, you telling me you are bowing out. Because I too am retiring and this young man is taking my place. This morning we're doing the rounds, introductions and all that".

The manager went on to remind me of our first meeting when the account was first set in place and we talked of how things had changed over the years until it was time for us to part, each wishing the other "all the best with our future plans". In the context of what followed this meeting and the pleasant conversational path of what took place is an important point.

On the heels of our advertisement in the Irish Independent I received three enquiries of positive interest. The first led to the quick sale of our smallest unit "The News Shop" at Powerscourt Townhouse Centre. The next biggest, also in the Powerscourt centre, attracted the attention of a man I knew fairly well. He enquired about the turnover figures and with that information said, providing his accountant was satisfied with audited figures, he thought the asking price for "The Main Shop"" was within his reach. However, knowing he was a man who had suffered with recent heart problems, I told him firmly that of all our shops this particular one, although profitable within our group, would take a lot of hard work for a solitary trader. My concern for his health was something I could not isolate from what probably should have been purely a straight business deal, between a man willing to sell and a man wishing to buy. The man thanked me for, as he said "being open and honest" and withdrew.

The third offer was the most interesting. This was for the "Mall Shop" beside the Westbury Hotel, a very busy and profitable unit.

The would-be purchaser was very keen on the outlet and told me of how his wife often said how much she liked it, adding that if it ever came on the market then that was going to be “her shop”. After several days of negotiations we agreed a price on the shop and for both parties to arrange a stocktaking exercise in order to reach a final settlement. The man himself ran a successful heavy plant hire company and a credit check confirmed he was more than equal to meeting the purchase price. Solicitors details were exchanged and as I believed, everything was going smoothly. How wrong I was.

The first signal of a hitch came when our retail manager Linda called me on the phone to say the our main supplier's local salesman advised her that we could expect no further supplies. In other words, the Camberly account was “on stop”. At once I got through to the firm and asked to speak to the senior accountant who regularly looked after the account only to be told he was no longer with the firm but that the sales rep. was on his way over to see me. A short while later the representative called. He was a nice person, someone who efficiently handled our requirements for quite a few years. The man was clearly embarrassed as he explained why supplies were stopped and this was his tale.

A day or two earlier his company was hit by some customer closures, resulting in extra-large bad debts. A hurried top-level management meeting took place during which all seriously overdue accounts were examined. Apparently eight customers were deemed to in that category and because the long serving accountant was too lenient in applying their credit terms on those who had closed and others near the brink of failure he was fired on the spot. As the meeting broke up, one voice asked “What about the Camberly shops ... they owe us a fair amount and are about to close”?

According to the rep. this remark set off alarm bells. That puzzled me. Having given their sales manager proper notice of my plans to sell the shops it now appeared as if we were on the verge of an immediate closing down and in current jargon "about to do a runner". When I stressed to the salesman that was far from reality, he shrugged his shoulders and replied the decision to halt supplies was not his. I realised of course, he was just the messenger and asked who I should speak to, confident that the supply matter could be quickly sorted.

My phone call to the supplier's financial director lasted no more than about two minutes. As I began to explain, telling of our advertisements to sell on the business and of my meeting with their sales manager, I was interrupted and told that unless the account was fully settled by Friday he would take steps to see Camberlys placed in the hands of liquidators. Even though we were a long standing customer I had never met the man who was now bluntly threatening to see a profitable business closed within days. To precipitate such a reckless action did not make sense. My immediate problem was that Camberlys had a 90 day credit term arrangement and that meant, at any one time there was a large amount of money due. A total sum which could not be raised in cash over a few days. After the telephone call events moved at breakneck speed. By lunchtime I was in discussion with our solicitor Stanley Siev who organised a meeting for the next day with the firm's accountants and a barrister. To have arranged the session at short notice was fantastic At the meeting a letter was drafted, containing an assurance from the solicitor that all debts would be settled on the pending sale of the Mall Shop confirming at the same time that he and the purchaser's solicitor had exchanged papers. The four of us agreed I should deliver the letter in person before three o'clock and seek a verbal response by 6pm. When I posed the question "What if they don't reply"?

The barrister said "Their swift actions are worrying and if they don't go along with what is a reasonable offer then you have only one choice and that is to beat them to the punch and liquidate the company before they do. Believe me, within hours, news of what is happening will spread like wildfire and your shop purchaser will step away from your agreement. You know how well the Dublin grapevine works, everyone, including your bank manager and other suppliers will fear the worst".

I couldn't believe how fast events were moving, so out of my control. I looked at Stanley Siev and before I could say anything, he turned to the barrister. "Knowing Roy this affair is a heavy blow to his pride, the position he's suddenly in, the idea of a liquidation after years of building an excellent retail business and a good reputation, is a bitter blow".

The barrister appreciated how I felt but repeated his earlier remarks. With that, he turned to the accountant "Should our offer be rejected or ignored, how soon could you arrange for a liquidator to move in"?

Again my breath almost stopped short when the man replied he would try to see such an action set in place by the coming Friday. I wondered aloud why a solicitor's letter of assurance, seeking a little extra time to meet all suppliers dues might not be accepted. One member thought, the pressure and threat could be an attempt to gain control of Camberlys, adding, "After all, the business is profitable, has an excellent image and if a large organisation injected further capital then it could be extended countrywide". There was nothing more to say or add and I hurried to deliver the important letter hoping with every step that it would result in a friendly acceptance.

By 5.30pm and with no come-back from the supplier the writing was on the wall. With not even the courtesy of a reply to a solicitor's letter, I phoned the accountant and most reluctantly requested him to get in touch with his nominated liquidator. It was an awful decision to take, one I believed was so unnecessary and forced upon me.

Early next morning, after I advised the staff of our situation, the would-be purchaser for the Mall Shop called in to see me. "I've heard a rumour about Camberlys". Before he finished I told him what had happened. Under the circumstances there was no way to proceed with our deal, leaving us and his wife no doubt, disappointed.

Coming on top of my still bereaved feelings, I found living with the added frustration and tension, a burden that literally weighed on my neck and shoulders. Fortunately, I never suffered with headaches but late one night in bed, tension caused my shoulders to hunch up, over my neck. Aware of what effect the recent pressures and stress might have on me I turned onto my back, stretched the spine and adopted a form of self sleep-inducing "mind over matter" drills.

There were still several important legal and business commitments to be cleared but with no cash income and money draining away at an alarming rate I was juggling with finances every day. To ensure everything was handled in an orderly fashion I sought extra time to meet the few remaining obligations and to this end almost 90% of those approached were understanding and cooperative. What was needed was the time to sell off assets, achieving the best prices and discharge all contracts. To say this was an uncomfortable experience would be a huge understatement.

Two uppermost concerns were the shop leases with years yet to run. As things stood we were obliged to meet the rents due until the contract termed periods ran out. As you may remember, when I tried on behalf of my Parents, to negotiate a lower lease surrender settlement figure on the toy shop I was told "We've got you over a barrel".

My first call was to Michael Doyle at the Westbury Hotel. I told him the whole story of what happened, placing all the cards in front of him. He listened intently, then said, "You've always been a good tenant and my father had a high regard for you, as I have. Whenever you wish to hand over the keys give them to our estate agent and that will be the end". We shook hands and I thanked him for the generous decision as he wished me well for the future.

The next meeting with Robin Power at Powerscourt Townhouse produced an almost identical response. He too commented on how well both our shops at the centre had been operated and that at no time during rental negotiations or other landlord/tenant meetings had I, as chairman of the tenants committee, ever adopted a confrontational approach to the discussions. He asked when I wished to hand over the keys and when I replied 'within days', he nodded and said "Just leave them in the security office".

It was a great relief to find two people with the same more than helpful attitude. Unlike my previous landlord encounter they were not going to put me over the proverbial barrel and I was and still am, all these years later truly grateful.

Another pleasant engagement that bowled me over took place at the Dublin Corporation HQ in Lord Edward Street. It happened like this: Every year, for the best part of 25 years, upon receiving the Corporation's business rates demand, I telephoned the chief accountant Mr. Murphy and after an amicable exchange of greetings during which we updated our annual news and views, I asked if he would allow our companies to stagger payments over three months, a proposal that he always accepted. It was a helpful ease to our general cashflow and a consideration we never took for granted. Although he and I had not met I somehow felt that we had, so friendly were our chats. When I called Mr. Murphy to advise him of our business closures and that this call to his office would be my last, he expressed sadness and asked if I would accept an invitation to meet him in person. Twenty-five years is a long time in business to know someone, even by telephone, sight unseen!

His greeting on the following morning was like that of an old friend. To my surprise, he was very like I pictured him in my mind's eye. A tall smiling slim man, in his mid-fifties, who led me to a large room, more like an old fashioned drawing-room than an office. His general well groomed and suited appearance reminded me of my school headmaster, Joseph Barron.

Soon after my arrival another man joined us. "Mr. O'Neill, this is Mr. Samuels, the gentleman I told about. He and myself go back a long way by 'phone and now, we're actually meeting for the first time".

My host was greatly amused and with the introduction told me that his colleague Mr. O'Neill was the Dublin City chief accountant. Minutes later, a large tea trolley arrived with a silver tea and coffee set, china cups, saucers and a fully filled cake stand. It was quite a sight.

Mr. Murphy laughed at my show of surprise. "We don't indulge in grand style like this every morning, usually its a mug of tea and plate of plain biscuits".

During our chat, an interesting fact came to light. Whereas in past decades the Dublin Corporation and Dublin Council bodies operated separate from government control, in autonomous manner, now the mechanics behind various tax raising methods were controlled by a higher authority and when I expressed more surprise, Murphy laughingly said, "Ah, now you are talking of the old days, when the Corporation was independent and ran its own affairs as it saw fit."

“And now”? I asked.
“Now we do exactly as we're told. The government sets the Dublin Corporation and Dublin County council rates. They tell us what they want and we comply. You are not alone in assuming that the money we raise is simply for covering Dublin's running costs. Oh no ... a large chunk goes into the national pot.

I got the impression he was a decent conscientious person, unhappy with the newer practices laid down by senior civil servants at the behest of ministers and looking forward to retirement day.

As for me, well Mr. Murphy, like an old friend wished me well for the future with a good Irish send-off. A non alcoholic send-off but a stylish and sincere one nonetheless.

The pleasant accounts described above reminded me of something my Brother Melvyn once said on hearing a story of bad behaviour. “Yes, there are some nasty and even evil minds out there. But remember, there are a lot more decent people around.

22

TEACHING A HORSE TO FLY

Most of us are familiar with tales of yore or good-old-fashioned sayings, containing advice on how to cope with problems and stress, pressures that assail us all at one time or another. In an earlier chapter I mentioned the book The Road Less Travelled by M. Scott Peck. As a reminder and to save you doing a rewind here is what I said;

The opening line (of M. Scott Pecks book) begins ...
“Life is difficult and proceeds to say that until a person accepts and comes to terms with that as a fact, then one is not in a position to deal with the difficulties facing them”. The author M. Scott Peck considers that the route and answer to coping is self-discipline and in accepting responsibility for one's own actions.

In addition to the much appreciated love and assistance I've received from Family and friends over the years, I've also been fortunate during tough times to draw on a fairly strong mental drive to grapple with life's raw deals. Different problems have been met with different, determined resolutions; from almost sublime reasoning to a cussed refusal to mentally buckle and when all else seemed inadequate, I fell back on one of my Father's 'Bubbameisters'

For anyone not familiar with the word the literal translation of Bubbameister is “grandma's fairytale”. The phrase is also used to scornfully suggest that a story presented as factual is no more than a Bubbameister.

So, having explained all that, let me tell you this story told to me many, many years ago of how one man dealt with a life threatening problem.

Way back in time, there lived a professional story-teller named Yankel. He earned a steady living travelling from town to town where the innkeepers housed, fed and paid him a modest fee in return for entertaining their customers with wondrous tales of faraway lands. To broaden his knowledge he decided to venture abroad to a country ruled by an eccentric king. Soon after his arrival, Yankel was mistakenly identified as a notorious thief and sentenced to death by the King. To await his execution, the prisoner was thrown into a squalid cell occupied by an old man. At once Yankel began to deal with his problem. Turning to the wretched convict he said, "Please sir, tell me about this king of yours. What sort of a man is he? For example does he have any special likes or hobbies in life"?

The bedraggled man thought for a moment and sighing sadly replied, "I'm afraid he has little respect or regard for anyone or much in life, except for his pet horse".
Yankel's eyes opened wide in surprise. "Horse did you say? The king is fond of this pet creature"?
The man nodded.
"He treats that animal better than any human on earth".
The storyteller smiled a thank you and moved to the cell bars where he called for a warden and gave the following instruction. "Take an urgent message to the King. Tell him that if he spares my life for six months, I'll teach his pet horse to fly". At first the warden refused to do as he was bid until Yankel warned him "If you fail to pass on this important message and the King later finds out there was a man with such great skills, who was executed because of your inaction, then you'll be next in line for the chop". With that warning the concerned guard rushed away.

Confident the King would release him, Yankel sat near the rails awaiting his release. In the far corner the cellmate called to him. "Thief or not, one thing is for sure, you are a madman. You know ...

and I know, you cannot teach a horse to fly. What on earth is going on in that crazy head of yours"?

Yankel grinned. "It's quite simple really. The way I see things are like this; right now I've got just a few days left to live. However, when the King hears of my offer and because he loves this horse so much he'll be intrigued and agree to the terms".

The listener interrupted him. "Yes, yes, so you get a six month reprieve. What then"?
The storyteller continued. "Well, as you have just said, I've got an extra six months to live and in that time certain things may happen. For example, who knows, during that period the King may die, in which case I'm free. Or, within that time the horse may die. If so the deal again is off and I'll be freed. It is also possible, through natural causes, I may even pass peacefully away - end of my problem".

The old man shrugged. "And if none of those things happen, what then"?

Yankel smiled once more and looking upwards, spread his arms wide and replied, "WHO KNOWS ... by the end of six months, perhaps I'LL TEACH THE HORSE TO FLY"!

23

BEING IRISH

If you're Irish, come into the parlour,
There's a welcome there for you:
If your name is Timothy or Pat,
So long as you come from Ireland,
There's a welcome on the mat.
If you come from the Mountains of Mourne,
or Killarney's lakes so blue,
we'll sing you a song and we'll make a fuss,
whoever you are you are one of us,
if you're Irish, this is the place for you.

Ah ... more fond memories come flooding back. At many a camp fire we scouts sat and gustily sang the above chorus from our large repertoire. As with many other frequently sung numbers the words have stayed in my mind.

On leaving Ireland in 1990 I was struck by the thought that, like my Family and me, many millions of Irish men, women and children have emigrated from a land they dearly loved. From the period of the Great Famine onwards it would be safe and not unkind to say that one of Ireland's biggest exports has been people. I've heard it said that if it wasn't for the Famine and the British government's mishandling of the crisis the Republic's population today would be closer to 9 million instead of the current 4.5 million and because the lower figure has not generated enough business opportunities within the island young students, skilled workers and would-be entrepreneurs have been enticed away to more populated places. Then, in the early 1990s a massive change of fortune took place. For a time, and on the back of huge hand-outs from the E.E.C. the 'Celtic Tiger's' heady decade of economic successes further mushroomed with overseas investments breaking the long dismal years of slow economic growth. The glory years came to an end in 2008/9 when the country was hit by what became known worldwide as 'The Crunch'.

Regardless of the reason or reasons for emigrating the Irish never seem to cast off their emotional connection to the 'ould' country. The leaving of Ireland may drift from single years to many decades, but the length of absence doesn't matter. To para-phrase Terry Wogan (among others) when he spoke of his native town Limerick, "you can leave Ireland, but Ireland never leaves you".

That may read strangely to some ... but stranger still is the enormous number of people around the World who claim to have 'Irish Roots', the majority of whom have never set foot on Irish soil! In the United States alone over 30 million Americans claim Irish ancestry. This past week (2009) Senator Ted Kennedy died. Almost every newspaper and commentator referred to his Irish/American family background. A couple of days later the ex-boxing champion, Mohammed Ali visited Ireland and called upon a family with the name O'Grady. The story is; his great, great, grandfather was an O'Grady. American President Reagan was another who claimed Irish connections, while at this time of writing it has been said that President Obama has green roots!

Even those who don't claim to have Irish roots are quite prepared to celebrate Saint Patrick's Day all around the globe. In Manchester for example, where we live, the build-up to March 17th goes on for two weeks and the centre city is swathed with green decorations; shops, pubs, restaurants, all join in the spirit of the occasion culminating with a street parade.

Why the desire of non-nationals to claim Irish heritage no matter how tenuous the link? It's difficult to explain. So is the fact that most emigrants, regardless of when they departed, have deep emotional feelings for the country of their birth. A close friend who left left Ireland 30 years ago, still tunes in each day to the Irish national radio station in order to catch the 1pm newscast. After an absence of thirty years one might reasonably expect the local news bulletins covering a much changed country would not relate to his previous awareness of people and events. This compulsion to keep in touch is in my view illogical, yet I respect and understand my friend's wish 'to stay in touch'!

As with some ethnic communities the Irish abroad, although they mix well and integrate easily with the wider community, can be quite clannish, but not in an exclusive way. When the Irish celebrate everyone is welcome to party with them. However, some will say that visitors to the green isle are greeted and treated well but are not expected to outstay their welcome. On a personal level, I have not seen any evidence of such behaviour. In a reverse situation, since our arrival in England the natives have been most friendly and we now live well integrated and happily among the Brits, as do many of our Irish friends. It is worth mentioning that between our Sons and 'selves, we know at least 300/400 Irish citizens who now live in Britain, mainly in Manchester and London.

The following chapter deals with the Family arrival to Manchester in 1989. It is now (2009) 20 years since that event and even though we came with strong past British connections on both Anita's and my side of the Family, we often compare notes on the differing forms of English and local expressions common to England and Ireland. For example, despite many reminders from our Sons, I frequently use the phrase “Please attend to that, and don't put it on the long finger”. To-date, not one English person has understood that sentence. Yet it's an old form of pressing for a quick response, such as, “Please attend to that, and don't put it on the back burner".

Collins dictionary under the word 'long' offers several meanings, including "'Long Finger' - To postpone something".

It is easy to understand where this particular old expression came from. Take a familiar saying, one commonly used on both sides of the Irish Sea, "Tie a knot around your finger" (so as not to forget something). Long ago the advice carried a tail-piece "and don't put it (the knot) on the long finger". The total message being remember but don't delay.

In Ireland everyone refers to the linen cupboard, where the immersion tank is usually situated, as 'The Hot Press'. Not so in Britain. On more than one occasion we have been challenged on why the Irish use such a strange name for a linen closet. Yet, here again is another example of an old English expression lost in the mists of time, but still used in Ireland. To a reader living in Britain, not convinced in what I've said, well look up a decent sized dictionary and you will find under the heading "Press", the following meaning; "large shelved cupboard for clothes".

I would be interested to hear from our Irish friends in faraway lands as to what different names are applied to things we grew up with in Ireland. To Benita and Zally Barnett in Australia, Vivienne Rosen in California, Elaine Bloom / Rose and Aubrey Yodaiken in Israel, "Nu"?

And to anyone not familiar with the expression "Nu" ... let me elucidate. It is a word you will NOT find in a Chambers or Oxford dictionary. A lot of Jewish people will greet their friends, Jewish or Gentile, with "Nu"?

This can mean “Hello and how are you”? Or - “What's new”? Or - What is the follow-up to our last meeting when we spoke of a health issue - a friendly business matter - the weather ...?
In fact, just as they say, 'There are 40 shades of green' ...
So too, are there 40 ways of saying “Nu”, at least!

There are many old English expressions still in every day use throughout Ireland, but long forgotten here in the U.K. In addition to all of that the Irish have a way with words, described by the late writer Woolf Mankiewicz, as 'colourful'. More than colourful, just think of the many great Irish writers, so many from a small country. Here are a few that come readily to mind; Edmund Burke, Brendan Behan, Samuel Beckett, Christie Brown, James Joyce, Patrick Kavanagh, Thomas Moore, Edna O'Brien, Flann O'Brien, Sean O'Casey, C.S. Lewis, John M. Synge, Jonathan Swift, Bernard Shaw, Oscar Wilde, W. B. Yeats.

Yes, some of these notable writers also crossed the Irish Sea, which reminds me of a funny comment made by Stephen Fry. Part way through one of the entertaining TV shows “QI” he turned to Irishman Dara O'Briain and asked:
“Do you know why the grass in Ireland is greener than England's”?
O'Briain guessed the answer might lie in heavier rainfalls.
Fry shook his head.
“No ... the grass in Ireland is greener because all the Irish are over here ... walking on our grass”!

Frequently, the Brits enjoy a laugh at the expense of the Irish. A quip over an Irish way of pronouncing a word, and so on. Well the joke also works the other way. What amuses the Irish is to hear every day and in all directions, including radio and television presenters say “I were stood there”, “I were sat there”.

NO, you were not. You were SITTING there or you were standing there, but please, stop with the sat sat sat in the wrong tense.

The other most abused expression is uttered when people part company. “I'll see you later”. Later? Like later when? Sorry to quibble, but there is a good parting word “goodbye”! Or, if you prefer Au Revoir.

Smile dear English reader, just a leg pull for Ireland.

24

FRESH FIELDS

With the coming of June 1989 Colin, Ian and Anita were now in our chosen new city of Manchester. Other than Colin's investigative visit weeks earlier none had any real knowledge of Manchester's districts. One or two ex-pats, now settled in the city, did warn them not to bother searching for living accommodation or work premises in what were termed 'rough areas'.

Our very good friends Shirley and Ralph Morris provided Anita and Ian and two family dogs! ... with beds and space for several days. The dogs an Alsatian and a Shetland Sheepdog were obedient and well trained but imagine, two big animals suddenly under your feet.

The dogs by the way were named Bob and Shanks after Liverpool Football Club personalities; the highly successful manager Bob Paisley, and the legendary manager Bill Shankly. Colin stayed with Gayle's parents; Vivienne and Aubrey who, also embarking on a family move to Manchester had just rented a house.

Within days of their arrival, Colin, with Aubrey's help, found a modest suitable business address, a combined office/warehouse rental on the third floor of an old cotton mill located in Ancoats, close to the East side of the city.

It was well that Anita quickly found a ground floor maisonette to rent in the Whitefield district. How Shirley and Ralph coped, I'm not certain, but they did so graciously. Looking back Anita, Colin and Ian seem to have accomplished miracles inside days. While Colin was programming a computer system, lining up suppliers, freight companies and overseeing workers who set office and warehouse units in place, Anita and Ian were daily opening fresh retail accounts. Within three weeks they had orders from Dillons and Waterstones bookstores from every corner of Greater Manchester, Merseyside and North Wales. Each day they telephoned to give me their good news, a much needed boost to my morale and confidence.

The new company was up and running, widening their network month by month, so fast it soon became necessary for Peter to join them ahead of schedule. This meant extra work for Neal and myself but as they say it was all for the common good. Meantime, I was delighted to learn that Camberlys senior manager, Linda Moore, had been hired by Waterstones main Dublin branch as Manager.

Years before the term 'Celtic Tiger' was coined, the property markets in Dublin and Manchester were quite similar. A house selling for £200,000 in one city could easily have been matched, like for like, across the Irish sea and marketed at the same price. This made it handy for us to evaluate what selling and buying strategy to adopt when it came to selling and buying properties in both towns.

While Neal, my Parents and 'self were still living in Dublin, Colin and Gayle announced their engagement.

Vivienne and Aubrey arranged a lovely evening party at the Adelaide Road Synagogue. As our in-laws-to-be had also taken the decision to move to Manchester it was clear that the wedding, planned for Saint Patrick's Day 1991, would take place in Manchester.

Colin & Gayle's Engagement Party
Neal, Peter, Gayle, Colin, Ian
Ma, Pop, Anita, Roy

Recently, 96 Liverpool football fans who tragically died during a semi-final cup match between their team and Nottingham Forest were remembered in various ceremonies throughout the UK. This terrible happening took place 20 years ago in April 1989 at the neutral venue grounds of Hillsborough Stadium, Sheffield. Minutes before the game began, the police, in order to ease the crowd pressure outside the grounds had the Sheffield club officials open the gates. Thousands of Liverpool supporters pushed forward, anxious not to miss the opening play. Their unchecked surge lead to people inside being crushed against barriers and walls.

Although at the time the police were cleared of blame the Sheffield authorities now admit, grave errors were made by the club officials and police. As a result of that tragedy standing terraces at all major football grounds in the UK were done with, replaced with banks of seats.

As the year progressed, so too did Ireland's football fortunes. Under the management of Jack Charlton, one time central team player for Leeds United and England, the Irish team made excellent progress to the quarter finals of the World Cup. Every game created immense excitement, with pubs screening the matches. I was drawn with Neal to watch along with both Peter and Ian who had returned briefly to Dublin to join the cheering throngs. The fact that the players could not hear the shouts and applause of encouragement did not dampen the locals' enthusiasm who responded to the play as if they were actually attending the game. Surrounded by the roaring cheers I soon got swept up in the fervid mood. After downing a second Guinness I was advised to speed up my intake a wee bit. Someone pointed to three more pints waiting for my attention. Having bought a round of drinks earlier for all the lads I once coached as juniors they were now in turn returning the favour. With more drinks to come, I reacted fast. There was no way I could down more than three pints in one evening so I quickly handed on the full glasses to willing hands, at the same time getting out the news that I had reached my limit, possibly the only one in the pub to admit to that.

Whenever the Irish team was scheduled to play an afternoon game Dublin virtually closed down. With deserted streets shops closed early, but the hotel bars and public houses packed to capacity. A recently arrived visitor walking the lonely city streets may have pondered long and hard about the Irish and their love of sport, and drink! Even I, having lived there for over 50 years never witnessed such scenes before, nor since, but have little doubt that a good run of performances by any national team in any sport would bring forth the same kind of public support.

By January 1990 two newly built houses were purchased in Salford. Anita and I bought a four bedroom detached home and in the same cul-de-sac, Colin moved into a similar four bedroom dwelling. I was still travelling to and from Dublin, spending every second or third weekend in Manchester and although family life was a bit dis-jointed, we managed over a twelve month period very well. On each car journey via Holyhead I managed to bring from Dublin our remaining personal belongings.

At the same time, in preparation for their move, my Parents began packing some of their small effects. My Father in particular, forever the optimist, was becoming quite excited by the prospect of a new start in life. After his retirement he continued to take an interest in how the Family's business interests were doing and soon he would get on-the-spot first hand reports and see for himself how the new venture was progressing.

Two miles from the newly bought homes and on the edge of Manchester Town sits Strangeways prison, the largest jail in the North-West. In April there was an alarming riot which rapidly gained momentum and threatened to get completely out of control. A large number of inmates led by three long serving prisoners broke from their cells and unable to break free of the prison set about destroying whatever they could. The main leader managed to get onto the roof and began throwing slates at warders and police below. During a lull, the convicts asked for a reporter to be allowed in to hear reasons that lay at the heart of their protest. Mostly the complaints targeted bad prison conditions. The men claimed that years of discussions had led nowhere and this new and violent outbreak was an attempt to bring the matter to a head for a satisfactory resolution. Eventually, with a promise by the governor to begin a fresh enquiry into the main grievances and a plea by the ring-leaders mother to end the protest, peace was restored.

It was about this time, when Ireland Plc began to apply for EEC grant aid. According to one tax official I met back then, figures compiled by that person's office were produced to make the Country's economy appear in a worse state than it actually was, in order to maximise the EEC hand-out. How true that was I couldn't say, I'm just quoting a civil servant. The individual further explained that the department was given figures by a minister and instructed to 'work back from the bottom line'! Years later I read that Italian government officials played the same game. I suppose someone might say those people responsible acted within the rules book, just as British M.Ps have done with their personal tax claims in the years to 2009.

Early Summer 1990 and it was time for my Parents, Neal and me to join Anita, Colin, Peter and Ian in Manchester. Neal wanted to stay on a wee bit longer so four of us with a few remaining personal effects squeezed into a Toyota Carina and headed to board the Stena ferry at Dun Laoghaire. It was the last time Da saw Dublin and although Anita and I returned with Ma many years later, a much changed city did not hold the same fond attachments we once had for the place. Our town and its surrounds were changing rapidly. In the stores, pubs, restaurants, immigrants were replacing what we called the typical Dub ... staff you could chat and banter with. Whether placing an order, or talking of the weather the friendly and witty come-back line had vanished.

Days after my arrival I called to the business premises at Ancoats where Colin was performing 'jack-of-all-office-functions' with some part-time helpers.

Off premises, Anita, Peter and Ian were all engaged on a magnificent strong sales drive. Although I already knew of the fine job they were doing it quickly became even more evident that with Colin at the helm excellent progress was being made. From a standing start-up, a completely new business had been formed; now operating successfully and achieving profitable results within a short period. I was so proud of what they had accomplished and wanted to offer whatever help I could without stepping on any toes. This did not come easily to me. As someone who managed a business for over several decades I initially found it difficult to perform a lesser role but gradually eased into a new post, that of credit-controller. In a growing business this position was soon placed in other hands as I moved on to become the senior accounts manager.

In Britain big political changes were about to happen. Margaret Thatcher in one of her last international appearances as Prime Minister, rubbished the idea of a single European currency, a European Central Bank, or of closer political integration. She actually placed the proposals as being in - cloud cuckoo land. Apart from Britain all the EC countries voted for a single currency.

My mind went back to the mid-to-late 1950s when the idea for a European Common Market was first mooted. The main emphasis at the time underlined the value of a large trading bloc and with a successful partnership (embracing in particular Germany and France) make the possibility of another armed conflict between the two countries less likely.

By 1990 many politicians, like Thatcher, were unhappy about closer unity with the EC and within the Conservative party ranks opinions deeply divided the Tories. Some political analysts say that gathering dissent had more to do with Maggie's overbearing style of leadership than issues concerning Europe. The same strong personality that broke the power of the miners union leader Arthur Scargill, reduced government spending, cut income taxes, and successfully handled the Falklands war waned under attacks from senior Conservative members. Michael Heseltine, Nigel Lawson and Geoffrey Howe were the main leaders behind the party rebellion. After winning three elections in a row Margaret Thatcher stood down in November and was replaced by John Major. In December, four and a half years after Prime Minister Thatcher and French President François Mitterand confirmed the agreement to build a Channel Tunnel the final block of wall separating England from France was broken through.

When it comes to evaluating Margaret Thatcher's performance as Prime Minister, with hindsight, people today are still deeply divided over her actions and achievements. Once in the driving seat at Number 10 Downing Street she embarked upon a radical transformation of Britain's economy. Big spending cuts were made in public spending as she strove to improve competitiveness. In time the high unemployment figures came down as the private business sector engaged more staff. In doing this Thatcher removed one of her biggest challengers the; Miner's Union. With careful preparations the Prime Minister broke the power of the unions in a swift and what some felt was a brutal manner and then set about privatizing much of the industrial state sector. More evidence of her strength of character showed through with her handling of the Falkland's war.

Despite Thatcher's critics ... and there were many, she won a third election in 1987. However, the Prime Minister's overbearing rule alienated many of her cabinet colleagues and eventually as she tired from the heavy workloads, they brought her down.

Personally, on balance, I thought Margaret Thatcher's actions were more beneficial to the nation. Great Britain, once commonly looked upon by most of the World as “The sick man of Europe” was now seen in a more favourable light and the ex-leader deserves much credit for that. By comparison, the majority of those who unreservedly criticised her achieved little or nothing.

The Tory party replaced Margaret Thatcher with John Major as leader and although he went on to win an election in 1992 (by a narrow majority) he lacked the strength of character to impress the electorate and build on that success. The economy was not doing well with rising bank interest rates and sinking property values. We had bought our new house at the peak of market rates, but having bought and sold houses several times we were not unduly worried. In our time we had seen prices rise and fall, with the long term graph always showing an upward trend.

25

Meeting Mickey, Donald, Goofy, Pluto and ... Groucho Marx!

In more ways than one many people will readily admit to never really having grown-up and I am one of that happy band. Childhood dreams of playing with model trains still beckon me to build a whole railway set, rolling stock, scenery, complete with buildings, vehicles and figures to scale.

It was our old pal Ralph Morris who suggested we join him and Shirley on a trip to Florida. Although he did say 'Florida' my mind immediately spelled out DISNEYLAND ... in larger letters than the ' HOLLYWOOD' sign overlooking Los Angeles. I didn't need any persuading nor did Anita who relished the opportunity to soak up some Winter sunshine. From the moment we assembled at Manchester Airport we smiled and laughed our way through the next 10 days. During that time, with our hired car, we got to see most of the theme parks including the Kennedy Space Centre, an amazing site. The Space Centre was just over an hours drive, a place we spent most of the day at. Our visit included a three hour guided coach tour of the premises including the actual launch sites of previous missions. Although we had seen several televised screenings of various rocket launches it is hard to grasp just how large the spaceships are. They are enormous. There are 5 burners at the base of a Saturn rocket and these are about six to seven feet in diameter (well over 2 metres) big enough for a person to stand inside.

An interesting aside. Bearing in mind the first moon landing took place on July 21st 1969 when Neil Armstrong and Buzz Aldrin walked on the Moon it is said that now, 40 years later, to repeat a similar mission to the Moon would require not only a new team of specially trained astronauts and technicians but a complete new development of spacecraft. That is unlikely to happen in the near to midterm future since President Obama declared in February 2010 that, due to national financial constraints, no plans for further Moon exploration could be entertained.

Still on the subject of space travel, in a recent radio discussion on BBC Four, a group of astronomers showed great excitement over new sightings of stars which may contain forms of life. Asked how long it would take earthlings, with present day rocket technology, to reach the nearest of these planets, one expert replied, “76,000 years”. Book your reservation now!

The publicity blurb for the 'Walt Disney World's Magic Kingdom' says: “The wishes and dreams of childhood fantasies come true”. If you haven't visited Disneyland with your child or grandchild then try and do so. To witness the expression of joy as they see all their favourite story characters come to life is something you won't forget. When we four adults made our way through the main entrance and I saw the familiar Disneyland castle Anita turned to me and said - “Take that silly grin off your face”. A sign promoting 'The Magic Kingdom' reads, “Imagine a world where you can fly with Peter Pan, dive 20,000 leagues under the sea, take a hitch-hiking ghost home with you and meet Mickey Mouse backstage in his private dressing room”. And apart from a young child's viewpoint, for the adult, that's what Disney is all about, once you are prepared to let the years roll back and allow your imagination run free it's a great long laugh.

For anyone who hasn't been, quite a few people buy a four day pass for the Disney Park and many find two days would have been sufficient time spent there. A lot depends on the time of year. On our visit the queues for the rides were short and so we got to see all that we wanted in a full day. For adults with small children and at peak holiday time, well, it ain't going to be that quick.

Nearby, well everything in Orlando is nearby, is Epcot, Another Disney theme park. The name 'Epcot' stands for 'Experimental Prototype Community of Tomorrow'. This place is more suitable for adults and the older child/teenager. Along with impressive displays/projects of tomorrow's world is a collection of towns, each representing a city of the world. There you can drink a beer in a typical British pub, enjoy a coffee beneath the Eiffel Tower or enter a Japanese pagoda.

A highly enjoyable trip was that to Universal Film Studios. At the time of our visit, it was the most recent of all the Orlando attractions. Among the theatres and special rides were street scenes depicting New York and various other towns. According to a guide these sites were used as back-drops for the making of TV productions, as was the special studio set-up for the popular long running series 'Murder She Wrote', starring Angela Lansbury. Wandering through the lot we came across staff playing the parts of well known stars. The impersonations were excellent and we couldn't resist having our photographs taken with Groucho Marx and Laurel & Hardy. I've included within these pages prints that still evoke a chuckle.

I suppose the reason for our great amusement is that Anita met Laurel & Hardy at Dublin's Gresham Hotel. They were then appearing at the Theatre Royal, the second largest theatre in the British Isles. In my case I never met the Marx Brothers, but as a youngster saw every one of their films. Their unbounded anarchic behaviour, similar to that of Chaplin, was brilliantly timed and aimed at pompous cruel characters. Comedian Spike Milligan and actor John Cleese admitted the humour of the old black and white films influenced their productions such as The Goon Show, Monty Python's Flying Circus and Fawlty Towers.

Yet another great centre of entertainment is Sea World. It is more than a giant aquarium. The big tank show with 'Shamu' the killer whale was in itself worth the entrance ticket. In addition there were seal shows and a massive glass lined shark pools to walk through.

In remembering these and other unmentioned themed places we visited, one overall impression is clearly stamped on a visitors mind. Unlike other Disneyland sites elsewhere the Orlando park is complemented with a host of other show areas. In fact, I would describe Orlando itself as one huge theme park.

26

A WEDDING DAY AMID A SEA OF SHAMROCKS

As we entered 1991 the date set for Colin and Gayle's wedding seemed to rush forward. March 17th, Saint Patrick's Day fell on a Sunday and the couple were delighted to be able to celebrate their big occasion on Ireland's national day.

Gayle's parents Aubrey and Vivienne, booked a large Synagogue reception hall on the South side of Manchester and hired a highly reputable firm of caterers while Anita and I engaged the florist, photographer and bridal car. The planning worked to perfection and the huge success of the event was due in no small part to Aubrey and Vivienne's excellent choice of venue and caterer. On the Friday before the Wedding our youngest Son Neal and I went to the Synagogue Hall with a large selection of Saint Patrick Day decorations. Some of these measured up to a metre in diameter and with dozens of green garlands and green white and orange Irish flags we spent most of the morning decorating the big reception hall.

Towards the end of our work spell the Synagogue Rabbi (an American and familiar with Saint Patrick Day celebrations) entered the hall with a teacher. As they gazed in astonishment around the massive display of Saint Patrick logos (within a Synagogue premises) the puzzled teacher turned to the Rabbi and said, “Why is all this Saint Patrick stuff in our hall”? The Rabbi replied “Ah it's just an Irish celebratory mishagas (daftness)”. I'll bet no other Synagogue anywhere, ever received a Saint Patrick Day make-over!

On the wedding day and shortly before heading to the nearby Synagogue, Anita and I paid a brief visit to our future in-laws home where Gayle was being prepared for the marriage service. She looked really stunning in white and I became quite emotional. Looking at this pretty young woman relaxing in an armchair was like seeing our own daughter about to marry and from that time on we have always looked upon Gayle in that light.

The marriage ceremony, followed by a reception, dinner and dance, was witnessed and enjoyed by over three hundred guests, many from Ireland and further abroad. Needless to say, apart from the Irish decorations, there was a strong Irish flavour to the whole event. When it comes to celebrations few can equal the Celts. It was a day for everyone to remember.

For another young couple, March 17th 1991 would also be forever remembered. It was at the wedding that Ian met his cousin Marcelle Lakmaker, the first time they'd met since early childhood. It is not for me to say what chemistry or sparks were ignited that day, but from then on the couple kept in constant touch. More of that story to come.

Back from their honeymoon in Paris and Amsterdam, Colin and his small team settled into a newly purchased office/warehouse unit in Heywood Lancashire. A recently built premises, Colin bought it at a bargain price and in time it proved to be an excellent investment. Still depending on goods purchased from the U.S.A. the wholesale business continued to thrive and by now Ian was opening new accounts in Europe. The first, a firm in Paris, still trades with the company 16 years on. Soon after another long supplied account was opened in Holland. At this stage Peter and Neal had joined Anita and Ian on the selling front. Colin, with a warehouse hand and me helping out with paperwork managed to keep things moving smoothly behind the scenes.

Although the business was still growing the sales team found it slow work opening new accounts, or as most suppliers to the retail trade call it “Cold calling”. Ian's summing up of the situation was in order for the company to expand at a faster rate participation in a few major trade shows would be necessary, an expensive but worthwhile venture he believed. Checking exhibition calendars, prices and space availability a booking was arranged for the Spring Gift Fair, a five day show in February 1992. The venue was (and still is) at the NEC Exhibition Centre on the South side of Birmingham.

Harold Lorsch the American supplier of humorous signs came over to assist and found selling techniques in the UK very different to the States, the British buyers being less open to 'pushy' selling. On the aisles it's one thing to invite passing visitors to view the goods on the display stand but Harold's loud jolly attack sent the majority of passers-by scurrying out of his path. After an hour of failed contacts, and feeling baffled, he turned to Colin with a laugh, saying “The English are kinda shy ... aren't they”!

Colin had to explain that generally throughout Europe buyers did not welcome the hard and fast in-your-face approach. Much to Harold's surprise when the trade show closed the firm's order book showed a good level of newly opened accounts and repeat orders from existing customers. Since then the business has participated every year in various UK exhibitions.

Outside of work the Family settled down well with new friendships. Anita found two groups of tennis players and from time to time I joined in what proved to be hard fought but very convivial matches. We also saw much of our fellow Irish ex-pats, most of whom left Dublin long before us. On a regular basis Anita and I continued to not only enjoy the company of our Family but also took steps to see friends as frequently as possible, especially during certain times of the year, like Saint Patrick's Day and New Years Eve. On every single occasion definitely without fail, our friends in London Dr.

Joseph and Joyce Levy, joined us in hail, rain and yes, even the heavy snows of 2010!

In December 1991 Colin, Gayle, Anita and I attended a gift fair at the Javits Exhibition Centre in New York. It was our second time attending this venue. The impressive waterfront building is a fitting tribute to a remarkable man who accomplished so much in a lifetime spanning 82 years. Not having heard the name before I was curious to learn more of someone who was highly regarded by New Yorkers and Americans across the States. Born and bred in New York, Jacob Javits, a brilliant student in law, wrote several books and was considered an expert in political and economic problems, a very wide field. When the United States entered the second world war he enlisted into the army and rose to the rank of Lieutenant Colonel. Returning to law in 1945 he joined the Republican party and served as a high profile Senator for 24 years. To mark his remarkable service during that time he was awarded the President's Medal of Freedom.

Unlike our previous visit to the New York show this one failed to ignite our interest in any of the goods on display. Sometimes that happens, but despite coming away with nothing in hand, there are positive things to be gleaned in attending. As I used to say on my return from such trips 'Although I did not bring back any new product, I was reassured to see we were up-to-date with our range and not lagging behind current trends'. That is an important point, to know that when dealing with customers, no one is going to say 'the selection is dated'.

Every once in awhile a mystery takes place that baffles everyone. For instance, the case of the 'Mary Celeste'. This was a wooden merchant ship of about 350 tons that was found abandoned in the Atlantic, off the coast of Gibraltar in early 1872. The vessel, sailing from New York, was in perfect shape but there was no sign of the Captain

(Briggs) his wife and young daughter, or crew of six. When another sea captain (Moorehouse) boarded the craft he got the impression the entire crew had left in a hurry with personal effects left behind. Down the years, books, films, and TV debates have expounded a wide, and sometimes wild, range of views on why the Mary Celeste was abandoned. With all that no-one has solved the mystery. One last point on this story. The author Sir Conan Doyle, creator of Sherlock Holmes, loved a good mystery and wrote about the sea puzzle. In doing so, he changed the ship's name to Marie Celeste. Why? That's another mystery!

As a young boy I saw a black and white short film with actors performing different presentations of what might have taken place. Like many people I've been fascinated by this event and as mentioned in the opening paragraph to this subject, every once in awhile a mysterious vanishing takes place.

Elsewhere in this book I've mentioned the disappearance of Lord Lucan and in 1991 another well known personality vanished. Robert Maxwell, owner of the Daily Mirror and New York's Daily News newspapers, was a man who seemed to have lived several lives. A flamboyant character, he was born in Czechoslovakia, became a British officer in World War II and entered politics as a Labour MP from 1964 to 1970. Thereafter, Robert Maxwell entered the world of publishing and became a millionaire in short time. On his way to financial success he made a host of enemies, mainly because of his brash bullying manner. At some stage during the early 90s, it seems Maxwell overstretched his business operations and to cover mounting debts fraudulently took £400 million from his employees pension fund. Against this background he went on holiday aboard his luxury yacht Lady Ghislaine. In the early hours of November 5th his body was found off the coast of the Canary islands. Whether he slipped from the boat deck or committed suicide no-one knows.

According to members of the crew, his behaviour prior to the incident appeared quite normal. So, as the years roll by, the Maxwell story will, as happened with the Mary Celeste, Lord Lucan and the missing racehorse Shergar, be looked at again and again prompting more wild speculation and fanciful opinions, adding to the riddle.

When living in Dublin we were in the habit of visiting the cinema fairly often with friends. The outings were part social, part entertainment and we always enjoyed the evenings. During our settling-in period in Manchester we seldom saw a film but slowly this changed. In 1991 the general run of productions was poor. However, we did get to see three very different kind of films that were entertaining. The most impressive was 'Silence of the Lambs'. The acting was superb and both Anthony Hopkins and Jodie Foster earned Oscars for their performances in the award winning film. On a completely different level we saw 'The Commitments', a picture set in one of Dublin's north-side tough areas. It captured the raw earnest efforts of a young band of poor musicians striving to succeed in the world of popular music. The director Alan Parker also allowed the cast to freely express their scripted frustrations in a vernacular common to that part of the city, with embellishing swear words taking the place of adjectives. Apart from the word “Bloody” I have never sworn but with our friends Shirley and Ralph Morris we laughed loudly at what we saw as typical Dublin scenes. Not everyone saw it that way and during our visit several people walked out with undisguised disgust.

Our third selection was a light comedy 'City Slickers' with Billy Crystal and Jack Palance. The latter earned an Oscar for best supporting actor, an award I feel given more by way of recognition of his time spent in the industry than for what was a lightweight performance.

As the year drew to a close British property prices fell substantially. Our recently bought house was now worth about 10% less than the purchase price but such is the way of economic cycles and something we'd seen before. As time proved house prices did rise and to a higher level than we had ever seen. From our first of several moves the market has moved like the tides ... first one way, then back again, but and this is the important factor, over a long period of time the overall trend is upwards. By the time we next moved the value of our property showed an increase of over 30%.

With business at the new premises in Phoenix Close, Heywood running smoothly, Ian began trying to widen our market share of CDs in Europe. Whereas UK sales were steadily growing with few credit risks the European scene presented not only the opportunity for faster growth but increased exposure to larger losses. The business took some time and a few big financial hits before establishing a more reliable credit checking system. Many credit insurance companies will openly say that country ABC or country XYZ are so dodgy to trade with that excess premiums are required and even then credit facilities to those areas may not be entertained. The common term heading used is "Oh, that country, along with a couple of others notorious for late payments and bad trading practices come into the 'Latin American category' and included in that sphere are places within Eastern Europe".

The nicest people you could wish to meet often prove to be the biggest con-artists. And that's how they succeed, working on well polished patter they quickly build up trust and credit limits, feeding suppliers with small payments in the early stages, while racking up large repeat orders.

When these foreign distributors went down, we turned to on-the-spot liquidators and solicitors for help. Having first established we were dealing with so-called reputable professionals, we were soon fobbed off with responses like 'No understand English'.

In each 'bad debt' case every possible angle for the recovery of monies due was tried including engaging an expert interpreter who forwarded full details of the debts, in the local language, without ever getting a single reply. It became clear after a time that either the customer was not worth the chase and/or the amounts owed were not worthy of their time and effort. The hard lesson learned was, with the exception of existing long established accounts, payment arrangements for all new overseas customers should be based on 'Pro-Forma' terms.

Fortunately, tight credit controls on UK sales meant that 'bad debt' losses were so minimal that a credit control and factoring company who offered a free quotation for handing the debtors list said “You don't need us”, something we already knew but it was nice to get an outside independent view.

The Queen described 1992 as her Annus horrbilis. It was the year a major fire destroyed a large section of Windsor Castle. The event in itself was upsetting but it followed another unfortunate blaze, surrounding the disintegrating marriages of Prince Charles and Prince Andrew. The tabloid press chased and harried the Princess of Wales and the Duchess of York, soon to be disparagingly referred to as 'Fergie' as rumours fed upon gossip, leaked tapes of intercepted telephone calls and a host of embarrassing photographs. Whatever fragments remained of the 'fairytale' marriage between Lady Diana and Prince Charles were well and truly ended with the sensational publication of Andrew Morton's biography of the princess, “Diana; Her True Story”.

Every week seemed to herald a new crop of royal media disclosures, with the tabloids in particular all out to capture the public's attention with more and more sensational headlines. Even the television news departments felt it necessary to join in the hunt, with in-depth interviews from almost anyone who claimed to have an 'insiders' slant on a particular new scandalous revelation. For the Queen and Prince Philip it was an embarrassing long-running saga with no let up through the year.

John Major who succeeded Margaret Thatcher as leader of the Conservative party and Prime Minister surprised most political pundits by leading the Tories to a win at the general election. As a result of the unexpected outcome Neil Kinnock resigned as leader of the Labour party. Liberal Democrat leader Paddy Ashdown also resigned his position but not because of the election result. His frank admission of having had an affair with his secretary actually improved his standing in opinion polls!

Meanwhile, and not for the first time the economy was in poor shape. Bank of England interest rates increased to 16% and by the Autumn Sterling was withdrawn from the European Exchange Mechanism. It was said then that one of the main causes for the collapse was to do with speculators undermining the Pound's value. George Soros, the American millionaire, claimed to have added many more millions to his nest egg by betting on the falling currency.

Adding to the pervading gloom IRA terrorists exploded a bomb in Northern Ireland killing eight Protestant building workers, then devastated a section of the Baltic Exchange in London, killing one person and injuring more than a hundred. Later, more IRA bombs were detonated in Manchester hurting over 60 people.

The IRA bombing campaign carried on into 1993 with terrible results. At a shopping mall in the town of Warrington two young children aged 3 and 12 were murdered when explosive devices placed in litter bins went off. The callous act provoked a wave of outrage and even some hard core Republicans tried to distance themselves from the murderous act. However the bombings went on. A large bomb exploded in the City of London killing one passer-by and injuring 40 others.

One of the worst crimes of murder in '93 had nothing to do with the IRA. The awful event happened in Liverpool when two boys aged ten kidnapped a two-year old toddler, separated from his mother inside a shopping mall. The two older boys murdered the child, James Bulger, three miles away, near a railway line. It was a crime most people found almost impossible to understand.

The case against the accused created a furious surge of moral contempt when they appeared at a preliminary hearing at a local court. Assailed by a furious crowd, the police found it difficult to shield the two boys and this resulted in further hearings being transferred to a court in Preston.

Rebounding from her horrible year of 1992 and possibly to improve the Royal image, the Queen took steps to contribute to the Exchequer, agreeing to pay income tax on her personal earnings. The Prince of Wales also made a similar commitment to pay tax on his earnings. Another milestone was reached when, in order to meet bills for repair work on Buckingham Palace, the Queen agreed to open the Palace to tourists during the Summer months. In time the Queen overcame the critical press comments regaining a large majority of the public's affection. As time goes by I see her gaining the same wide fond respect her mother received over a long period.

In contrast to the previous year the cinemas in 1993 drew in larger audiences with a host of excellent films. Topping the list was

'Schindler's List', a remarkable film produced and directed by Steven Spielberg. The film tells the true story of a German business man named Oskar Schindler, who during World War II, saved more than a thousand Jews from certain death at the Auschwitz gas chambers. This amazing brave man managed to rescue prisoners by claiming he required them for his factories helping towards the country's war effort. The part of Schindler is well played by Liam Neeson and among the other fine cast members are Ben Kingsley and Ralph Fiennes. A moving epilogue features actual survivors and families along with Schindler's widow filing past his grave in silent tribute. Steven Spielberg, himself a Jew, says he was driven for years to make this film. His long term desire being to ensure the Holocaust is never forgotten. The film gained two Oscar awards; Best film of the year and for Steven Spielberg, Best Director.

Other successful films were;
'Unforgiven', a tough western with Clint Eastwood and Gene Hackman.
'Sleepless in Seattle', a romantic fantasy, starring Tom Hanks and Meg Ryan. 'Remains of the Day'. This popular film could also be described as a romantic story but in no way similar to 'Sleepless'. With outstanding performances, Anthony Hopkins as a butler, and Emma Thompson a housekeeper, engaged at a mansion in the early 1930s or thereabouts, overcome the formal stiff trappings of relationships in that period.
'Jurassic Park' Another picture by Steven Spielberg with excellent special effects. In this tale of an amusement park where dinosaurs have been recreated, experiments get out of hand and the prehistoric monsters run amok. The cast includes Richard Attenborough, Jeff Goldblum, Sam Neil and Laura Dern.

We never got to see 'The Piano' with Holly Hunter and beautifully shot in New Zealand.

'Scent of a Woman' starring Al Pacino who won an Oscar for his performance as a blind man captivated by the scent of a woman he cannot see.

Two moderate but entertaining films we did get to watch were; 'Mrs Doubtfire' with Robin Williams in drag and 'Manhattan Murder Mystery', directed by and starring Woody Allen and Diane Keaton.

Looking back, it was probably one of the best years of the decade for the cinemas.

27

CELEBRATIONS

Earlier in this book, I wrote about Colin and Gayle's Saint Patrick Day's marriage in 1991. Among the guests were Anita's cousin Simone, husband Gerry, daughter Helma and husband Andy, also their younger daughter Marcelle.

Now although Anita and I on brief London visits saw Marcelle from time to time, she and our son Ian had not seen each other for many years. When they did meet, it was, as all best romantic tales describe 'Love at first sight'. At Colin and Gayle's wedding reception they danced the night away and promised to keep in touch on her return.

Two years and two months later we attended their wedding in London. On the Saturday before the big event we invited our ex-pat friends to join us for an evening at the Cumberland Hotel at Marble Arch. Over dinner we caught up with mostly news from Dublin, something we seldom get today as many have left the city for foreign parts. Unfortunately my Parents could not make the trip south. With Ma feeling unwell my Father would not leave her on her own for an entire weekend. Next day, the 16th of May, Ian and Marcelle were married in a London Synagogue. The ceremony was followed by a lovely reception at a city hotel and among my fond memories of that night were -
The blissful couple in a complete whirl of happiness; dancing, singing and on stage playing (sort of) imitation guitars!
Colin's wife Gayle, who was now 8 months pregnant, bouncing around the dance floor, including joining a wild Israeli dance, 'The Hora' and giving Colin, her parents Aubrey and Vivienne, Anita and I, palpitations.

And ... a very lasting memory, still fresh in my mind, was of the couple, at the end of the evening walking from the ballroom and as they did so, Ian removing his jacket to reveal a large (Liverpool) crest of the Liver Bird and the slogan “YOU'LL NEVER WALK ALONE”. A lovely appropriate touch.

At Ian and Marcelle's Wedding
Colin, Peter, Roy, Ian, Neal

Less than four weeks after the happy event, the birth of Tony. Colin and Gayle's first born entered our lives on Thursday 2nd July. My Parents, known to our Sons as Pop and Ma were thrilled to bits, as were Anita and myself. Living close to Colin and Gayle also placed us in line for baby sitting, an undertaking we proudly took to with no qualms.

Once more Anita and I became familiar with the trappings surrounding a new baby. The scents of powders and lotions recaptured as we happily enjoyed our new Grandchild. There is a phrase in Yiddish which describes the emotions we felt it is 'Schlepping Nachos' and the nearest translation I can offer is 'Drawing much Joy'. Now I'm afraid that does not really do justice to, or highlight the joyous feelings ascribed to that saying.

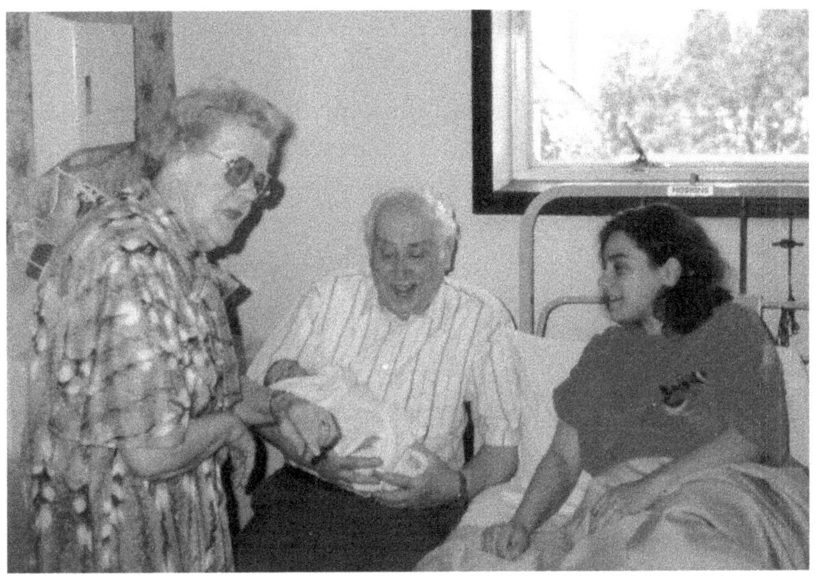

Ma, Tony, Pop & Gayle

In earlier chapters I've written of our enjoyable business trips and holidays to different cities and resorts. These covered a wide number of countries and without exception left us with pleasant memories. The places we visited ranged near and far, covering most European countries, North, South, East and West parts of the U.S.A. Russia and Israel. Having said that, with no bad experiences to tell, some of our favourite holiday destinations have been to areas within the U.K.

Towns like Bath and York stand out but our most popular haunts are the Lake District and Cornwall County. I cannot count and tell how many times we have stayed at the Cumbrian Lakes. It is a place we never tire of and have often spent weekends and day trips there with family and friends who know or are unfamiliar with Windermere and its surrounds. At any time of the year there is much to be enjoyed in the County. Most hotels - and we've stayed at quite a few, are good value for the rates charged. As the saying goes 'you get what you pay for'.

People often refer to the Lakes as 'Doggie friendly', meaning that in a large number of hotels and visitor centres, dogs are allowed, not necessarily within the hotels (although in some cases they are) but nearly always permitted on the hotel grounds. In shopping areas it is common to see outside shops 'hitching posts' for pets and filled fresh water bowls, a thoughtful gesture welcomed by dog owners.

With or without a pet doggie, if you haven't been to 'The Lakes' then do so as soon as possible. Celebrate an anniversary, a birthday or as the 'Mad-Hatter' said “Celebrate a non-birthday”. You've got at least 364 of those in a year!

28

1933, 1993 COMPARISONS

At this point of my reminiscences covering sixty years I am struck as most people of my generation are by the changes in life style since the 1930s. During that length of time the changes have been gradual. Many city and town tenement slums have disappeared and despite recurring recessions over intervening decades, living standards have improved immensely.

In book One 'Sailing Through Plate Glass Doors', I told of how on the streets of Dublin and Liverpool, where I grew up, a common sight in the Summer was that of young children going barefoot and of the various charitable groups who raised money to buy boots for the needy. Government led social handouts were virtually non-existent. In 1934 the writer J.B. Priestly made a tour of England and published an account of his journey. In many areas he saw gangs of unemployed men in cloth caps hanging around the streets of derelict boarded-up towns and declared the 1930s as “a decade of unrelieved misery”.

Unemployment rates in the worst towns was as high as 70%! Those who received unemployment money and who were commonly termed “On the dole” received about a third of the average working-class wage. This hand-out lasted for 26 weeks only, after which time those seeking assistance were 'means tested'. Further benefits were only granted in cases of extreme poverty.

It was during this period the 'Sweatshops' thrived. The name 'Sweatshop' derived from the slum factories in London's East End. Here, as in other cramped and damp buildings workers toiled for long hours and meagre salaries. The dreadful conditions, like those of the poorest unsanitary living areas, were breeding grounds for diseases such as tuberculosis.

Paradoxically, for the upper class in Britain it was also a time to earn a lot of money. On the backs of low paid workers large profits were made from the manufacture of goods sold to more prosperous middle classes. For them goods were fairly cheap. So too were places of entertainment, such as cinemas and dance halls.

Cinema prices were low so even those on low incomes could afford to seek comfort and refuge from the prevailing hard times. Musicals with Fred Astaire and Ginger Rogers, Broadway styled spectacular dancing routines choreographed by the legendary Busby Berkeley, comedies featuring Charlie Chaplin and the Marx Brothers, helped lighten the patron's mood.

For children there were special Saturday morning matinee films. The most violent of these were 'Westerns' or sometimes called 'Horse operas'. Cowboy pictures, as I knew them were pretty tame when measured against present day flics. Children could always quickly identify the 'goodie' (or 'The Chap' as we called him). The hero wore a white Stetson and the 'baddie' a black one.

In those pre-racially correct times we had 'Cowboy and Red Indian' films where the Indians were almost always portrayed as murderous scalp taking villains. The plot endings, so similar each time, found the brave cowboys sheltering behind a circle of wagons surrounded by fast riding yelling Indians, until a bugle is heard, and into sight to the rescue come a troop of U.S. Cavalry. At this point every kid in the cinema cheered their loudest.

Think ... there was no television then, no hand held games or money for expensive playthings and believe it or not kids were seldom bored. Girls and boys made up their own games, played mostly outdoors, or joined a youth movement. For me it was the Scouts. One thing I cannot understand is why the Scouting authorities found it necessary to allow girls to join scout troops. The Girl Guide association was specially created to cater for them. This is not a sexist rant, just a puzzlement as to how the change came about.

The Girl Guide movement celebrated its 100th anniversary on February 2nd 2010. They are obviously still going strong, without boy members so, once again, why do some girls join the Boy Scouts?

For the vast majority of children in the 1930s and '40s schooling ended at the age of fourteen. Few parents could afford 'secondary' level costs. A rare number of children managed to gain scholarships to high schools and colleges and those successful pupils I remember went on to become doctors, dentists, legal experts, or professors in some scientific field.

Recently (in 2010) Michael Portillo, an ex-minister in Margaret Thatcher's Tory cabinet fronted a TV programme that made comparisons with the British railway system of yesteryear compared to present times. In an excellent well produced documentary, Portillo, with an old copy of 'Bradshaw's Railway Guide' travelled the length and breadth of Britain on a series of short journeys, making comparisons, interviewing people to hear of their travel experiences before, during and post World War II.

Some seniors who worked in the coal mines or cotton mills told of how with their one weeks paid holiday money they headed to the seaside and for millions the seaside meant Blackpool, a heaven on earth. However, a week in heaven was followed by an unpaid second week, then another wait of seven days before the next pay day came around. Compare that with today; much longer paid holidays, travel abroad and think of how many cruise line ships are now in operation.

When my Mother reached her 90th she expressed a desire to spend a weekend in Blackpool. I suggested other places but no, Blackpool it had to be. A booking was made with the Hilton Hotel and to their credit, when I explained about the birthday wish the manager laid on a lavish reception. Ma received a great reception with a lovely room, champagne, fruit bowl, chocolates, flowers, and a dining table sited in what the head waiter called “Our best table for a special guest”.

My Mother was delighted, however certain aspects of the visit were less savoury. On a walk along the sea promenade a naked man came running towards us, chased by a gang of well-wishing buddies in what we discovered was part of a 'stag celebration'! Later, a group of young women played out a similar scene with an almost! naked bride-to-be. At this sighting, Ma declared primly “Blackpool is not what it used to be”. Inwardly I smiled, thinking; Blackpool was never what it used to be.

For those of us living in Dublin our youthful seaside holidays were taken mostly in Bray, County Wicklow, just 12 miles from the capital. It was a resort thousands flocked to, especially during the World War II years. To a lot of people then Bray was often described as Ireland's Blackpool. In no way did it look similar. Although much smaller in size, it had a lot going for it. All along the seafront hotels enjoyed a boom period and local residents with spare rooms to rent made handsome tax free profits. On the esplanade small kiosks did a roaring trade in ice creams, buckets and spades, beach balls, sunglasses and hats. There were boat rides across the bay, coach tours, rowing boats to hire, mini-golf, a fun fair and open entertainment on the band stands, Punch and Judy ... it was bonanza time. Bray buzzed with activity, but alas when the war ended, so too did the flow of visitors. By 1993 all the hurly-burly of a lively vital seaside resort had vanished.

In drawing comparisons with earlier times one hears conflicting views on whether they were 'the good old days' or times to forget. For me, as a young child in the 1930s with no responsibilities, I can cherry pick some golden moments, but am under no illusions what life back then was like for my Parents. It was damned hard work.

Politician Ann Widdicome in a recent television series to do with religion remarked on how she believed falling church attendances were leading to a lowering of morals. Her views were based simply on this, “Moses and the Jews were given the Commandments by God and these were later accepted by followers of Jesus as the foundation of Christianity”. On the other hand, Stephen Fry, on the same programme argued that the Commandments were not relevant and in fact were the cause of conflict down the years the world over.

I'm not certain of the point he was trying to make. This was probably because he became quite agitated in his discussion with Widdicome. In casting aside the Commandments he didn't seem to offer any ideas on what society should adopt as a code of behaviour for the masses.

In earlier writings I have mentioned what life was like during the second world war, both in Dublin and to some degree, in Liverpool. They were dark times ... six years of a bloody conflict that saw 6,000,000 Jews murdered among a total of 60,000,000 souls killed, mainly because of one German leader's quest for power. Adolph Hitler.

Can we rank the biggest hate monger of the 21st century, Osama Bin Laden, alongside the vilest individual to have walked on planet Earth? Perhaps if Bin Laden had the same power base as Hitler he might equal or surpass his evil record. In writing this piece I'm reminded that just now, 27th January 2010 is Holocaust Memorial Day. Millions of people around the world will take time out to remember the men, women and children slaughtered by the Nazis.

In the 1947 when I left school at the age of 14 to work as a factory apprentice the working week consisted of five and a half days 48 hours. This was common practise in all major industries, which by law had to abide by Government set working conditions. Gradually the hours reduced to 44 and by the 1960s, 40 hours. Summer holidays, generally taken in July/August lasted two weeks. Apart from that workers received another five days off during the year, which included Christmas. New Year's day was a work day, so anyone with a hangover from the previous night's celebration either carried a sore head into work or lost a day's pay.

Someone once declared “The more things change, the more they stay the same”. I'm not sure what the writer had in mind but I feel there are few things from 1933 that compare with 1993. That is not to say that every difference has been one of improvement. Some changes like advances in the field of medicine, to take but one example, have been of tremendous benefit.

It is interesting to listen in on other 'senior' opinions when present time behavioural and living standards are contrasted with yesteryears'. Views may be influenced by a media hyped report, highlighted in exaggerated form to command more viewers and readers, but one way or another we are all drawn to express our opinions on whatever changes have taken place. Even the weather can produce heated exchanges. The Summers were warmer/colder ... the Winters were colder/milder.

Usually, in a Saturday edition of the 'Daily Telegraph' there is an interview with a well known personality. Apart from answering questions on their likes and dislikes they are also asked; “If you had a choice, what period in time would you like to live in”?

An interesting question; amazing how keen many people felt about living in what we might describe as the romantic 'Bronte' age, ladies in crinoline frocks, corsets, gentlemen in top hats, tails, breeches and riding boots. Draughty, cold, candlelit mansions and medical standards that would horrify a GP today. And that was for the wealthy citizens. As for the other unfortunates ... ?

Years ago, my Brother Melvyn and I were making similar comparisons. He too could cherry-pick wonderful golden-oldie moments but after a lengthy chat he ended by saying, “Overall ... was life in general better or worse 50-60 years ago? You know, there really is no definitive answer to that. I suppose all we can say is, it was different.”

For myself, I am happier living in the overall living conditions of recent times than those of previous decades. Just as the song 'The best of times' goes...
“Live and love as you know how,
And make this moment last,
The best of times is now”.

29

THEREAFTER A COLLECTION OF SHORT STORIES

Having completed between these book covers 28 chapters recalling my reminiscences of the years 1973-1993, I felt someone might say 'For the sake of recounting a few more years of happenings and a few more pages, why not bring the story right up to the present date?'

Well ... I did think at one stage I might ... just might ... write a fourth book, but as I'm working flat out and painting and wanting to write a novel (a thriller) and ... still dealing with leukaemia, attempting to teach a horse to fly (reminder, see chapter 22), I thought ... here's what I'll do:

I'll add an extra chapter or two covering the years 1994-2010 with a brief, on the lead up to the Millennium and the following decade.

The day of 'Good Friday', Easter April 1994 was not a good day in the Samuels calendar. Just before noon my Mother telephoned to say Da was sitting in an armchair, awake but unable to move or talk. I immediately suspected he had suffered a stroke and asked her to dial 999, adding I was on my way. The ambulance and I arrived together and the moment I saw my Father I knew my guess was correct.

After a brief spell in hospital and when the medics confirmed there was no hope of him walking again we arranged for him to be transferred to Heathlands nursing home. This is part of a large complex in North Manchester called Heathlands Village. Set up by the local Jewish community it embodies residential accommodation for senior citizens. With that facility conveniently available we were able to book Ma into a small on-site apartment. This made it possible for her to visit my Father each day, helping him recover his memory more quickly.

The most newsworthy event of the year was the opening of the Channel Tunnel. From May 6th 1994 Britain ceased to be an island. Queen Elizabeth and French President François Mitterrand inaugurated the 31 mile (50km) rail link with the Queen travelling on a Eurostar train to Coquelles in France. On the return journey the President joined the Queen in her Rolls Royce aboard the train. One might say that was one-upmanship!

When I wrote above about the most newsworthy event of the year and the Tunnel, I was not including Family affairs. Our big news of the year was the birth of a second Grandchild. Ryan Samuels who decided to arrive way ahead of schedule. In fact Master Ryan was eight weeks early! I remember standing in the hospital with Anita peering into what looked like a plastic container. Inside, swaddled in a soft cover was the tiniest baby we had seen. Pretty soon, Ryan, with great nursing attention began to gain weight and strength bringing relief to Parents, Grandparents, and all the Family.

I was glad that my Father had the pleasure of holding his new Great-Grandson several times before his death in early 1995. His passing did not come as a shock. Sadly his body gradually weakened and a day before the 25th January we said good-bye to one another. I loved him dearly and look fondly upon a Father/Son relationship with not a single regret. My late Brother Melvyn and I adored him. He came from a poor (financial) background, but one rich in culture and the ways of learning. Throughout his life he rose most mornings at 6am for work and despite tortuous varicose veins I never heard him complain once. This may seem like a huge exaggeration, but of all the people I have met and known I never met a happier man. He loved people and he loved life.

Two years after our Son Ian's marriage to Marcelle they announced in '95 that Marcelle was pregnant. On September 30th Jessica, our first Granddaughter arrived. Along with the rest of us my Mother was thrilled and kept repeating; “A girl in the Family ... a beautiful girl”.

Anita and Roy with Jessica

As for the rest of that year, well I don't remember much worth recalling. Into 1996 and there were a few happenings that made news. Prince Charles and Princess Diana divorced after a 15 year marriage that probably went well beyond its sell-by-date.

They had in fact lived very separate lives for four years and although adultery could have been cited for the breakup, the actual grounds for the decree absolute was based on their official separation of 4 years. Immediately the press speculated on how long Prince Charles would wait before planning a wedding to Camilla Parker Bowles. Some day in the future a film studio is going to make a colourful film based on his and Princess Diana's love entanglements.

Two years after the Channel Tunnel opening, a section was devastated by fire. The damage caused by an electrical fault was quickly fixed, but between that and other problems that crop up from time to time, I am very reluctant to travel down the underwater tube. For example; what bothers me is when I hear, after each mishap, passengers say staff appeared to have no training for assisting travellers in breakdown situations. The 'Eurostar' rail company is owned by three firms, that could explain a lot!

One big disaster affecting the whole of Britain happened when Health Secretary Stephen Dorrell admitted there was a link between 'mad cow disease' and the fatal for humans disease CJD. Within days British beef was banned all over Europe. Many consumers in Britain also stopped buying meat. This was no surprise since the press reported several dozen people had died from contaminated meat. It was a dreadful time for farmers as millions of cattle were culled. The terrible thing was the problem appeared to stem from the practice of feeding cows with offal from slaughtered animals. Now, although my Father was a master butcher, I never laid claim to knowing much about cattle but cannot understand how anyone could think such a method of feeding would produce healthy meat for human consumption. As a vegetarian I'm probably too biased to comment any further!

About this time there was a television advertisement which for many viewers summed up the entertainment business. The scene was of a man sitting behind a desk unwrapping a bar of Kit-Kat chocolate. Sight unseen, he appears at the same time to be addressing some would-be stars; “You can't sing ... can't dance ... can't perform ... you'll probably go far”.

Overnight single artists and groups came along a conveyor belt of young and handsome performers. Talent didn't matter as much as appearance. It was like the old fashion trade joke 'Never mind the quality, feel the width'.

It's always easy for those of my generation to criticise present day standards, but who can honestly say levels of comedy and singing have improved. By comparison other areas in entertainment have shown improvements such as TV documentaries, drama, stage productions and the cinema. Mind you, the films of 1996 were on the whole disappointing. The best of a so-so bunch of forgettable films was 'The English Patient'.

In 1997 a dear friend passed away. I first met Sydney Bloom when I went to work as an apprentice at his father's business Alfred Bloom Limited, a manufacturing furriers. Sydney was 16 and I, 14 years old. Coming from different backgrounds it took a few years for us to find common ground. That happened when he joined what was then called 'Rover Scouts', later renamed 'Venture Scouts'. I had been a member of the 16th Crew for some time and he heard me talk of the great weekend camping we enjoyed at the cabin site in Powerscourt, County Wicklow. From then on we shared many good times together.

When I think of Sydney the word gregarious springs to mind. He was the most outgoing, affable friend you could wish for. To family and friends alike he was generous, warm spirited and fair in his dealings, whether in private matters or in business. We frequently paired when playing tennis against pals Monty Ross and Aubrey (Yoddy) Yodaiken. The twice weekly games, if not played in classic fashion, were certainly classic comedy. I doubt if anyone enjoyed or laughed as we did with Sydney contributing much to the banter. He could extract humour and see the funny side of most things in life. With wife Elaine, Anita and I, we frequently went on trips or dined out and regardless of the conditions we had a ball. Once, upon arrival at a hotel in Gran Canaria, a hassled receptionist claimed we had no reservation despite our confirmed booking form. It became clear they had overbooked and Sydney seeing little point in prolonging our protests, advised the clerk we would instead book into the most expensive hotel on the island at his hotel's expense. This we did and to our delight all our charges were met without a hitch.

Leaving the hotel that first evening and despite a disappointment that may have dampened any holiday, our spirits remained high. Sydney having dealt quickly and efficiently with the problem joked on our way towards hailing a taxi. Under a darkening sky, while Elaine and Anita stood on the pavement luggage-minding, Sydney with one trouser leg rolled up, tried to attract the attention of speeding drivers who seemed hell bent on getting home early. Eventually one taxi stopped and Sydney enquired; "Do you know where the Victoria Hotel is"? With a big smile the man replied "Si" ... and drove off. Sydney fell to the ground laughing.

When you have lived with, or known someone well over a long period there is no need to over emphasise or express in detail your views on most subjects. Longevity makes it possible to communicate in what becomes like a form of short-hand English. Even with humour, a knowing look and a single word synonymous with an incident or character from the past is enough to create a smile. Illustrating the point Monty Ross told this story many years ago:

“A group of friends were telling jokes over a drink one evening. Eventually one of the gathered circle said 'hey guys, do you realise that every joke we've told is one we have retold again and again. I want to make a suggestion, to avoid the long winded lead to the punch line, we'll number all our jokes. Then, when anyone mentions number 29 we can all relate and laugh'.

Everyone thought this an excellent idea and for the next few nights they all listed, numbering their favourite jokes. A week later the same band of friends met again, this time joined by a newcomer. One of the old pals said 'Remember this oldie ... number 42'? With that his buddies fell about nodding and laughing.

The newcomer was very puzzled by this but said nothing until near the end of the evening. During a lull in the conversation he said aloud, 'How about number 42'? When nobody even smiled he turned to the man beside him, 'How come, when that man over there said '2', you all laughed, but when I said '2' nobody even tittered'. His companion sagely replied, 'Ah yes, but you see we all laughed because of the way he tells it'!”

I tell the above joke to underline how at times Sydney and the rest of his friends created humour from the sublime to the ridiculous.

A major political turnabout took place in British politics when the Labour party, now freshly re-branded as New Labour swept into power with a large majority, after 18 years in opposition. Tony Blair, the new Prime Minister aged 43 promised to maintain Margaret Thatcher's controls on tight spending, union interference and still manage to hold his Labour left-wingers in check. And the public bought his package with both hands giving Labour, sorry, New Labour the biggest House of Commons majority since World War II. Here, before my Sons jump all over me, I have to admit, I too swallowed New Labour's promises; low taxes and Chancellor Gordon Brown's undertaking to exercise Prudence (with regard to spending). I don't know how many times he uttered that word prudence. As with the Pound, he devalued it.

On Sunday morning, the 31st of August, the bedside radio came on, as it did every day at 6.10. Before I could reach out to switch it off an announcer broke into the usual programme of light music, reporting news of Princess Diana's death. Early accounts confirmed she had been involved in a car crash. It was stunning news and rarely has the British public shown the kind of sorrowful emotion it did throughout the country. In 1997 Diana (regardless of her divorce) was still one of the World's most prominent celebrities. A high profile charity worker, romantic trysts with well known people including Dodi Fayed, son of the Harrods owner, who also died in the accident. I've used the word 'accident' when some people immediately claimed Diana had been deliberately targeted by a hit-driver!

Conspiracy stories surrounding the crash have never really gone away despite several thorough accident inquests. Each report stated there was no evidence to support Mohammed Al Fayed's claim that the British Secret Service were behind a plot to have her and his son killed.

During 1998, in the space of five months, our Family grew with the arrival of two lovely Granddaughters. Ian and Marcelle introduced us to their second child Jemma, who today as I write this piece, is celebrating her 12th birthday. Jemma and her cousin Ciara, Colin and Gayle's daughter, are now preparing in 2010 for their coming Batmitzvah ceremonies.

In the late 1990s as we headed towards the end of the 20th century people speculated on what the new millennium might bring. One big scare that gathered pace centred on the computer world with concerns that the change of dates would in some way collapse most systems. It was a great time for the computer service industry when nervous users arranged to have their equipment checked for possible breakdowns!

Apart from computer concerns, mother earth spun without too many major worries. In Ireland, green and orange politicians came eventually to talk peacefully to one another under what has become known as 'The Good Friday Agreement'. For the citizens especially of Northern Ireland who suffered years of bloodshed this was an auspicious time.

Before the century drew to a close our Family had one more event to celebrate; the wedding of our youngest Son Neal to Kath, a pretty young lady from Southport. Both ceremony and reception were held at one of the resorts' leading hotels, a place where we, along with many of our guests stayed the weekend.

Neal & Kath's Wedding

The couple had been engaged for over 12 months and leading up to the big day we got to know Kath very well. For Anita and me it was not only great to see Neal so happy but to also gain a Daughter-in-law who got on well with everyone else in the Family.

My Father always laboured the point of how important family harmony is and I try to follow in his footsteps. There are more than enough tribulations in the wide outdoors without building some more on the home front.

30

THE NEW MILLENNIUM

A time of fresh hopes ...

In company with close friends Joyce and Joseph Levy, Margaret and Milton Jeffries, Hubert Weiner, Vivienne and Aubrey Noyek, Anita and I welcomed in the new Millennium at home. The year heralded not only a new millennium, but also a change of home address (for the 11th time) and big changes for our Sons business.

The UK celebrations with its main focus on London and Edinburgh was brightly highlighted on television. Centre of attention to begin with, was of course 'Big Ben' bonging out the midnight chimes. Dozens of cameras then swung into action with well rehearsed shots of the new huge sightseeing wheel the 'London Eye', the equally new 'Millennium Dome', Tower Bridge and the Thames embankment. A massive galaxy of fireworks showered over all these crowded focal points. Similar colourful scenes of the Sydney and Paris celebrations were shown and I can still vividly remember the Eiffel Tower, layers of fireworks exploding from the bottom to the top very impressive.

Doom-mongers who warned the new millennium would result in massive global computer breakdowns were proved wrong. Where do these so-called experts disappear to? The British government, acting on 'expert advice'! had spent millions to counter a threatened bug that never saw the light of New Year's day. Days later life went on as before.

When I wrote above 'life went on as before', that was true also of family matters. Anita went house hunting again! And our Sons moved their business premises from Heywood to the Salford Quays, a few hundred yards from the new 'BBC Media City'. In addition to the workplace move, other important developments took place. The company, for the first time, began to produce its own branded music under the label Global Journey. This was a huge step forward and made it independent of any ties or dependency on music suppliers and within a short time 'Global Journey' compact discs were retailing throughout the UK and many EU countries.

In the Summer of 2000 a terrible air accident took place when an Air France Concorde crashed shortly after taking off from Charles de Gaulle airport. Somehow, as the 'plane sped down the runway a fire broke out below a wing. The pilot tried to land the aircraft on another airfield but failed to reach it, crashing into the town of Gonesse. All 109 crew and passengers were killed plus 4 people on the ground. Two years later British and French Concordes were withdrawn from service. The supersonic era was over and as I write in 2010 there is no new replacement of its kind on the horizon.

Our first Grandchild born in the 21st century arrived on the 2nd of November. Eoin a fourth child for Colin and Gayle, presented Anita and I with a new experience. At that time, having sold our home, we were living under the same roof with them. Fortunately their spacious home accommodated the new baby and ourselves comfortably. It was a lovely time and for months, until our new house was ready, we enjoyed all the excitement and activity that comes with a new arrival.

Sadly, my Mother never really got to know her latest Great-Grandchild. At the beginning of 2001 and after suffering a few falls she entered hospital but at the age of 91 her recuperative powers failed.

Ellen Elizabeth, known to everyone as Nellie, was a strong disciplined character. My Brother and I grew up in a home that was orderly: good manners expected at all times. For Ma, as we called her, there was no middle way. Things were either right or wrong and wrong was never acceptable. Even when times were financially hard and both she and my Father struggled to keep heads above water, life in the Samuels household seemed to Melvyn and me, always sound and secure. Da always credited Ma for being a good house manager, an excellent cook, good at handling money and good at looking after the welfare of their two children.

Some people who never got to know her well thought of Nellie Samuels as an unbending, aloof kind of person, probably because she had no time for those she could not trust 100% - the same black and white standards applied with personal relationships. However, although her emotions were more controlled than my Fathers', there were never any doubts of her love for him, her Sons or other Family members.

9/11
NINE ELEVEN

Whatever way you say it or print it, those numbers will forever be linked to one of the worst murderous actions ever.

It was a bright sunny Tuesday in Manchester and New York. At sometime during the early afternoon and as I entered the directors office, Colin called me over to his computer screen.

“Take a look at this ... a 'plane has just crashed into one of the Wall Street Towers”. I stood over his shoulder as the BBC newscast kept showing repeated shots of a large aircraft hitting the tall skyscraper. It was weird ... uncanny, with all of us in the office huddled around the computer, wondering how such an accident could happen in broad daylight. It wasn't until minutes later, when a second liner exploded into the second tower that the words 'terrorist attack' were used. More than 3,000 people perished on that morning. It was an unforgettable experience. It was immediately evident that Islamic extremists were responsible. Some political analysts began long winded explanations as to what was the specific reason for this assault. Too many people seem to think that Islamic terrorists are responding to what they believe are anti-Muslim actions. After 9/11 the London bombings, Madrid, Bali and those in Pakistan and India, panels of Middle-Eastern political observers pontificated on the reasons for each outrage. Few seem to understand the 'West' are engaged in a war. Not like that in Iraq or Afghanistan but a war of hearts and and minds. A vast number of moderate Muslims would agree with this.

On the night of 9/11 I heard on BBC radio 5 channel an interviewer ask an American, “Why do you think the United States deserved this action”? It was such a crass and insensitive question, I'm surprised the American retained his composure. The BBC man then likened the United States position with that of the Jews, as viewed by the Nazis and questioned what the Jews did to bring about such a hatred that lead to the Holocaust. Such ignorance.

In March 2002 one of Britain's favourite Royals; Queen Elizabeth the Queen Mother died peacefully in her sleep at the age of 101. The title 'Queen Mother' was specially created in recognition of her services to Britain and the Empire.

Two other notable happenings took place in 2002. In January twelve of the EU countries adopted the Euro as their currency. Gone was the German Mark, Franc, Guilder, Lira, Peseta, the Irish Punt and so on.

The second big event was the 'Queen's Golden Jubilee'. The 50th anniversary of the Queen's accession to the throne was celebrated with a series of spectacular events with concerts, fireworks and royal processions. The enthusiasm that greeted the Monarch throughout the days of celebration showed clearly how popular she was.

About this time, during the early Summer of 2002, I was playing a lot of tennis and began to suffer what I thought was a pulled arm muscle or a case of 'tennis elbow'. My local G.P. advised I get some massage treatment but after three months of expert attention there was no improvement. It was felt that something more serious was causing me problems. A blood test was recommended. I remember vividly how the events of that week unfolded.

The blood check was on a Tuesday and on the following morning I received a call from the doctor's clinic to say that an appointment had been arranged at the North Manchester Hospital for me to see Doctor Jane Robertson in the Haematology department, the next day, Thursday. All I could find out on the telephone was that my various blood counts were low and I was anaemic.

At the hospital more blood tests were taken and after what seemed a long wait Doctor Robertson saw me in her office. Without any flannel she came straight to the point, saying; "Mr. Samuels, you have leukaemia".

It was not something I was remotely expecting to hear and my shocked mind reeled, tumbling flashes of pain. It was as I have described in previous times, like walking into a plate glass door 'bedang'.

Many times I have heard people say on being told they had cancer, "Why me"? It's a natural reaction and those same words raced through my mind also. My immediate thoughts were for Anita and our Sons and the rest of the Family. I sat for seconds trying to deal with a host of unasked questions before saying, “How long do I have”? It felt so odd uttering this, almost as if someone else was speaking. The doctor did not answer the question directly. Instead she said, “I've made arrangements for you to come into hospital tomorrow, to begin chemotherapy treatment. This programme will run for several months”. Suddenly, the idea that there was some medication available to help me fight this terror lifted my hammered spirits a little.

An hour later at the Global Journey offices I gathered Anita and our Sons together and gave them the bad news and as calmly as I could assured them I would fight this damned disease every inch of the way.

Colin gave me a searching look. “Apart from the hospital treatment, what is your mental approach going to be”? “I am going to adopt the 'Red coat' tactics seen on the film ZULU”. A film showing how a small unit of about 120 British Redcoats fought off thousands of Zulu warriors. In no way should those soldiers have managed to survive but with massive determination they overcame massive odds. It was a vicious engagement, during which a Welsh regiment earned 13 'Victoria Crosses'. Never before or since has that number of bravery medals been awarded.

That same evening Colin came to our house and handed me a package. Inside was a Video Cassette, a copy of the film ZULU! “Watch this tonight to refresh your memory and get yourself in the right mood for what's to come”. Next day began a very long series of tough medication.

I won't dwell on the hospital events of the five internment months that followed except to to say:

1. The doctors and nurses were very helpful and sometimes when I hear people moan about the NHS it annoys me. The vast majority of hospital staff do a wonderful job.
2. My Sons equipped my private room with a Video Cassette player and a laptop so I could tap into all aspects of what was going on in their business. The room looked more like a business office then a hospital room. As Doctor Osbourne said one day when bringing around a medical team, “And this place, we call 'The Office', in fact I'm thinking of redesigning mine on similar lines”.
3. I cannot tell how many 'get well cards' I received, a staggering amount. On top of that the moment I got through the 'isolation' period the number of visitors was flattering.

Of course, every single day for five months Anita, Colin, Peter, Ian, Neal saw to it that one or more of them called in.

By November the chemotherapy had rolled back the leukaemia and I went into remission. It was tremendous news. I knew the menace would return but hey, it showed the disease could be floored by the 'ZULU' philosophy! and chicken soup! Or as many Jews call it “Jewish penicillin”.

31

A DISAPPOINTING END TO A DECADE OF HOPE

In one of the most controversial military actions involving American and British forces, Iraq was invaded in March 2003. The dictator Saddam Hussein was considered a danger to world peace. Responsible for the deaths of many thousands of Kurds and Iraqi citizens, the reviled leader boasted of his plans to produce atomic weapons, or as he described 'weapons of mass destruction'. Yet a lot of people were opposed to the invasion. Now, as I write this seven years on, the controversy still continues.

Briefly, some of the main news items that hit the headlines from 2004:
In February 2004, 21 Chinese workers were drowned while cockle picking on sandbanks in Morecambe Bay. The Chinese, mostly immigrant workers had all come from the Fujan province.

Then in April the village of Boscastle was destroyed by a flash flood. The disaster occurred 52 years to the day after the infamous Lynmouth flash flood in 1952.

After many years of a romantic liaison Prince Charles married Camilla Parker-Bowles in April 2005.

On the morning of July 7th, at the height of the rush-hour, Islamic suicide bombers detonated three bombs on the London underground and another on a double-decker bus killing 56 people. Once again there were people who found reasons to justify these horrendous acts, with remarks such as “Well you can understand that the U.K's involvement in Iraq has alienated many Muslims who feel the need to perform violent acts of what is considered revenge”!

In my first book I wrote of the world recession in 1933, the year of my birth. Over the decades more recessions and financial meltdowns followed, with the worst in living memory which began in 2008. The effects of this crisis are still being felt in 2010.

About this time my old enemy, leukaemia retuned and over the next four years Professor Yin, Doctors Osbourne, Rowlands and their teams have steered me through several trials. Now, Colin and the above medics are searching to see what other drug/trial options might be available.

For the future? Well I still battle with leukaemia, although day to day I seldom give it much thought beyond keeping my important meetings with medical specialists Professor John L Yin and Doctor David Osbourne. As I said in my Introduction, I owe them and the nurses at North Manchester Hospital, the Alexander Hospital and Manchester Royal Infirmary a big Thank You.

In the past year I have painted more canvases than in any previous year, written more words and with the exception of overseas travel and tennis restrictions, done most of what I wanted to do. Next I have to decide on what further paintings to line up and whether to embark upon one of three novels, plots that are burning inside me.

EPILOGUE

Following a fall Roy suffered a Haematoma, leading to a build up of pressure in the brain. He slipped into a coma and died on 11 April 2010. Shortly afterwards Anita found the below handwritten lyrics in his wardrobe:

Goodnight sweetheart, 'til we meet tomorrow
Goodnight sweetheart, sleep will banish sorrow
Tears and parting may make us forlorn
But with the dawn a new day is born

So I'll say goodnight sweetheart, though I'm not beside you
Goodnight sweetheart, still my love will guide you
Dreams involve you and in each one I'll hold you
Goodnight sweetheart, goodnight

Ray Noble - Reg Connely - Jimmy Campbell

Roy Samuels 14 August 1933 – 11 April 2010
Sadly missed by his wife Anita, sons Colin, Peter, Ian and Neal and grandchildren
Tony, Ryan, Ciara, Eoin, Aoife, Jessica, Jemma, Keiran and Rory

www.ingramcontent.com/pod-product-compliance
Ingram Content Group UK Ltd.
Pitfield, Milton Keynes, MK11 3LW, UK
UKHW020130250726
13967UKWH00002B/576